For: Sue

GILD

Mary Rochford was born and grew up in Dublin. She has spent most of her adult life in Birmingham where she read English and History at the University of Birmingham for a B.A. (Hons). She obtained an M.A. Literary Studies at University of Central England and has worked as a lecturer in Further Education. She has two sons.

Sláince!

Mary Rochford

October 2008

Mary Rochford

GILDED SHADOWS

Tia Publishing

First Published by Tia Publishing 2008
37 Chesterwood Road
Birmingham
B13 0QG

Copyright © Mary Rochford 2007

This book is sold subject to the condition that it shall not by way of trade or otherwise, be lent, resold, hired out, or otherwise circulated without the publisher's prior consent in any form of binding or cover other than that in which it is published and without a similar condition including this condition being imposed on the subsequent purchaser.

ISBN 978-0-9557810-0-1

Printed by Fast-Print Network
Graphic House
First Drove
Fengate
Peterborough
PE1 5BJ
United Kingdom

For my sons

Contents

Part I

Gilded Shadows -Trilogy:

The Silent Scream	11
Dreams of Salvation	28
Ashes to Ashes	50

Part II

Coming Home	73
Guardian Angel	89
Significant Moments	100
A Fresh Start	112
Cold Comfort	128
Something to Tell	144
Aftermath	156
Somebody's Son	166

Part III

Interlude	187

PART I

Gilded Shadows

The Silent Scream

The Atlantic was at it again, rumbling and heaving, thundering its fury into the night. The autumn gale whipped the ocean into great walls of water that rose higher and higher before toppling onto the beach below. As I peered through the misty window the moonlight played on the foaming waves and conjured a pale figure, pitched and thrown in the raging sea. Shivering, I drew the curtains and climbed into bed, pulling the covers over my head, trying to block out the ghostly image. I curled into a ball and rocked myself to sleep.

The wind, moaning and wailing between the gaps and slits of the cottage, jolted me awake. I tried counting sheep — god knows there were enough of them in these parts: counted the fine things of my acquaintance — done in two seconds. And still I couldn't sleep.

I pulled on my dressing gown, stumbled to the kitchen table and sat huddled over a bottle of Jameson's. To my right, through the open door of the adjoining room, a blank canvas glowed in the dark. I stared at it for a few seconds, poured a generous measure of whiskey and downed it in one. My escape to the edge of the world hadn't worked: memories and half-memories shadowed me, ready to pounce without warning. Getting unsteadily to my feet I shut the door with a resolute bang before putting Shostakovich's Seventh onto the turntable and setting the volume at very loud.

After the third malt I didn't care about the storm, the canvas or the past.

*

The early-morning sea lay calm and still, exhausted from the outburst of the previous night. Giddy from lack of sleep I snuggled into the warmth of my sheepskin coat —the bleating things have some uses — and stumbled across the wet sand. Rusting oil-drums, sodden driftwood, tangled coils of rope, bits and pieces of fishing line were scattered along the strand. Mounds of seaweed cowered in the silver light. The going was heavy so I slumped onto a tree trunk that lay stranded on the deserted beach. Through gritty eyes I looked out to sea.

*

My father, shirtsleeves and trouser legs rolled up, was digging for rag-worm on Sandymount Strand and I was holding his jacket. I was seven years old and as he worked he talked to me about fishing, how, as a boy, he'd hung around the men who fished the Barrow. In time, they'd allowed him to use their precious rods; showed him how to bait a hook and cast a line. He would run with his catch, a gleaming brown trout, and present it to his mother to cook for his father's tea. Occasionally, these men would take him to Hook Head where they cast their lines from the giant rocks as they fished for mackerel. As he recounted the story he stopped digging and rested his foot on the spade. He looked down at me, the pleasure of the memory lighting his face, and I was treated to one of his rare smiles.

I pressed my bare feet into the sand and sank slowly to my ankles in the grey mud. I dragged one foot out of the swamp and it made a great, sucking sound like one of Aden's rude noises. 'Daddy, tell me a story: the one about King Lir,' I demanded, glancing along the beach past the driftwood left by the tide where my brother and sister ran and shouted, circling again and again, the island that was my mother.

*

Ravenous after my early morning walk I dunked a slab of griddle-bread into rich, dark coffee and stuffed it in my mouth. My mother would have a fit if she could see me. But she wouldn't be seeing anything anymore; she'd passed away a year after Daddy; couldn't live without him, apparently. 'Died of a broken heart,' according to Biddy O'Driscoll. 'A load of blarney,' I say. It wasn't the loss of Daddy that killed Mammy; she didn't love him enough for that. The only one she really cared about was her darling Fionuala. It was Fionuala's dash to England that did for Mammy. I'd stake my life on it.

The Silent Scream

The door between the kitchen and the studio was as I'd left it the night before; tightly shut against the pristine canvas — the spectre that had been haunting me for weeks.

Three weeks previously I'd been ready to start the under-painting when Paddy 'The Slug' Griffin arrived, clutching a letter in his soft, bulbous hands. 'Just the one for you today, missus,' he said, brushing his oily fingers against my hand as I reached for the envelope. 'It's from Dublin,' he said, with a knowing smirk, 'the city where the girls are so pretty. Just like yourself. You're looking only gorgeous. That duck-egg-blue shirt is grand with your red hair,' he jabbered on, before stopping for breath and adding, 'and how are you yourself?'

'I'm busy, Paddy.'

'Not too busy to give a man starvin' with the hunger and dyin' of thirst a bite to eat and drink.'

'Never too busy for that, Paddy.'

An hour later Paddy, having devoured a bowl of leek and potato soup, a couple of slices of soda-bread and a generous measure of Jameson's to fortify him against a biting north-westerly, took his leave and left behind, not just the letter, but also an abandoned painting.

But the storm had helped. It blew away the turmoil that had started with the arrival of the letter. At last I was keen to work.

Leaning against the wall, the canvas glowed like fresh snow in the dim light. After the early morning promise the light outside had turned a sullen grey. To make the most of what was left I arranged the easel at a forty-five degree angle to the north-facing window, hauled the canvas onto it and mixed the colours for the under-painting. I selected a two-inch from the battalion of clean brushes laid out like surgical instruments on the paint-spattered table. I steadied the nervous tremor of my hand, loaded the brush and daubed the bluish–grey undercoat onto the blank surface, marvelling as always at how quickly the rough texture swallowed the paint.

As I worked the world outside the window dissolved and floated away in the swirling mist.

*

A mist hung low over Killiney Bay and trapped the heat of the earlier sun. My father was holding his fishing rod and was about to cast into the sea. He raised his right hand, swung it backwards then forwards, sending the silver line soaring above his head into the deep water. I was nine years old and I sat to his right, at the top of the steep shelf that fell away to the blue-green sea, my sketchpad resting on my knees as I tried to draw the outline of Bray Head. As Daddy prepared his line he talked about the grandmother who'd died before I was born. 'She had a story for every occasion,' he said. 'She believed the chattering of the pebbles was the voices of families clamouring for the return of their daughters who'd been lured away by the lord of the sea.'

I looked towards the horizon, hoping to spot the mail boat as it started its journey to England. Glancing along the beach I saw that Fionuala had escaped Sorcha and Aden and was running towards us.

'Your grandmother believed that the sound of the waves was the sound of sea-maidens keening for their loved ones. She was a great woman for the old tales,' my father said, and laughed. He looked at me for a moment before adding, 'You're just like her, Aefe; you have her wonderful, glowing hair.'

Fionuala's soft, podgy knees knocked against each other as she stumbled and staggered, but she kept coming. 'Da, da, da, da,' she called, but Daddy didn't hear her. Her infant legs failed and she fell and rolled towards the greedy sea.

Daddy turned to me, a smile playing round his lips as a memory formed that he was about to share, but he dropped his rod and ran, shouting foolish things. 'Don't panic, Fionuala, hold on, keep your head up. I'm coming, Daddy's coming.' He thrust himself into the tumbling foam, grabbed her and lifted her high into the air. He tore at the buttons on his shirt and clutching her wriggling body close to his chest wrapped her in the sodden garment. He walked away from me to my mother who was waiting with outstretched arms.

The waves crashed against the beach and dragged thousands of clattering stones into the deep water.

*

'Your obsessive interest in all things aqueous is enough to put any man off,' said Paul 'The Shit' O'Brien before he slung his hook and left me rattling round the house in Foxrock. A few months later, as I sat in the darkest corner of Bewley's about to scoff my second éclair and third coffee, Elis Murphy sidled up to me.

'Can I join you, Aefe?' she asked, smiling broadly. Without waiting for an answer she plonked herself on the seat opposite. 'I can't tell you how much we all admire you,' she said, her gaze riveted on the oozing cream and rich chocolate. 'Following your heart like that. Not waiting for the wedding ring. But sure haven't you been blessed with the free spirit of an artist.' I wiped the sticky sweetness from my fingers, looking beyond Elis's head to the pink hue of the stained-glass window. 'Men are so conventional,' she said, her flat face twisted with concern. 'Sure it was probably best that Paul and Aisling went abroad to get married. I'd love to get married in Rome, but then wouldn't any Catholic girl die for the chance?'

Quarter of an hour later, as I stood on O'Connell Bridge waiting for the traffic lights to change, I realized I'd left the restaurant without paying the bill.

*

Paul's trip to Rome wasn't a complete disaster. The sight of the pontiff must have kicked a guilty gene into life. He gave me some of the proceeds from the sale of his house in Foxrock, so three years ago, just after Daddy died, I bought the cottage, the car and all the canvas, brushes and paints that I could cram in the boot. 'I'm stifled by Dublin,' I said. 'I need space to pursue my work. I owe it to myself to find the place where it can flourish. I'm off to the West.'

'Your woman's flipped,' said Aden, the brother who'd never forgiven me for being the eldest. 'She's not safe to be let out. We should have her sectioned.'

'Good riddance,' said Sorcha, the sister who'd always wanted to be a boy.' The West is welcome to her. Anyway, if we fancy it, sure won't it be a good place for a cheap holiday.' As usual, Fionuala said nothing. She stood winding a tendril of blonde hair round and round her finger: her eyes large and wary. It took all my strength not to slap her sneaky, little face.

*

That first summer in Clare I wandered the wild coast in my gleaming new Mini and set up shop wherever the fancy struck. I spent summer days blinded by the sun as it soared above the ancient splendour of the Cliffs of Moher. Perched on top of Loop Head, I tried to capture the crimson and yellow ball of the setting sun. Occasionally, too restive to work, I hired a boat and sailed the Shannon Estuary. As the boat cleaved through the water the salt spray masked the tears that ran in rivulets down my face. On days when the mist rolling off the Atlantic shrouded the land in a dim twilight I stayed in bed.

The longed for letter announcing a visit from Sorcha and her brood, or Aden when he was on holiday from the navy, never came. After two years of waiting anxiously for Paddy's deliveries I gave up hope. And then, a few weeks ago, there he was, looking slyly from underneath his bushy eyebrows, and handing me what I'd been waiting for. As he slurped his soup and drank his whiskey I willed him, just this once, to deviate from his normal speeds of dead-slow and stop. When he finally left, my hands trembling, I tore at the cream envelope addressed in Sorcha's looping handwriting. Two sheets of paper fell to the stone floor. One was from Sorcha, but the writing on the other was unfamiliar. I glanced at the signature and was shocked to find that the faint scrawls, sliding off the page, were Fionuala's. Clutching the sheets of paper I moved towards the window to catch the grey, mist-drenched light and read Sorcha's brief note and Fionuala's short letter.

Looking past the privet hedge towards the ocean I saw my father's tall figure as he was about to cast his line into the sea and heard his voice. He was talking about his mother. 'She was a wise woman, your grandmother,' he said. 'She only offered one piece of advice that I remember. She would say to me, "Be careful what you wish for, Con, for you might get it".'

*

A routine developed after the arrival of the letters: I drank whiskey, fell into a drunken sleep and dreamed.

I float from the bottom of the sea, drifting upwards until the silent, watery world recedes and leaves me stranded in the middle of a vast expanse of sand. A tiny figure stands at the water's edge. Instinctively, I know it's my father. Between us, close to a great mound of rocks stands my mother, a colossus with dark hair reaching to her waist. Slowly, she glides away from me towards Daddy, clutching a small body to her breast. Although I am running like the wind, I make no headway and I can't get past her. Like a flying fish, Daddy soars through the air and appears full-sized beside me. I lift my hand, desperate for his reassuring touch. But in an instant he's gone, dragged back to the water's edge, a minute speck beyond my mother. I try with all my strength to reach him, but I can't move. I look imploringly at my skinny legs, willing them to run. But they're not there. In their place a fish tail flaps wildly on crimson sand.

*

When I started working again the dreams stopped. Pleased with my progress I decided to treat myself to a night out at The Armada.

'I suppose we're trying to emulate The Royal Academy,' Theodore Yeats said. He'd come west for the fishing and his rotund figure was propped against the bar as he sipped brandy. 'We've decided to mount a Summer Exhibition. We want to give the cream of Irish talent the exposure they deserve.'

'And what Royal Academy would that be, now?' asked Paddy 'The Slug' Griffin, licking porter from his fat lips.'

'The Royal Academy, London of course,' said Theodore, delighted with the sound of it.

'And there was I thinking we could manage our own affairs these days,' sneered Paddy. With a great sucking sound he drained his glass, banged it on the bar and staggered from the room.

'It seems I've upset the natives,' Theodore smiled. 'Anyway, as I was saying, our exhibition this year is premised on the mythology of the Irish seascape and, from what I've been hearing about your work Aefe, we may be able to hang one of your paintings.'

*

The Sea Maiden's silver-green cloak billowed in a great arc as she slithered down the cliff towards the ocean. After years on dry land she had found the magic garment and was making a dash for freedom, clutching her infant to her breast. Above the crashing waves, Muireann heard the pounding of Finbar's feet on the cliff-top, but she kept going — one backward glance and her cloak would lose its magical powers and all would be lost.

I lay on my stomach reading The Myths and Legends of Ireland which Daddy had given me for my tenth birthday. My mother was crouched low, kneeling on the fine, dry sand of Seapoint strand, helping Fionuala take off her clothes. Aden and Sorcha were struggling into their swimming costumes. 'Tell them to stop kicking sand all over me,' I cried.

'We're not doing anything, we're just getting dressed,' they whined.

'Aefe, take Fionuala for a paddle in the sea,' my mother commanded.

'I will in a minute,' I said, playing for time and reading on. Muireann clambered over rocks until she

The Silent Scream

reached the water's edge. She steadied herself, preparing to jump into the foaming waves when a terrible scream rent the air.

'Do as you're told, now, Aefe.'

'In a minute, I will in a minute.' The chill, green water called to her, but the searing anguish of the cry forced her to turn and look at Finbar one last time and that look sealed her fate. The sea rose in a great wall of foaming water, and swept her and her daughter into its murky depths.

'Take your nose out of that book, now, and do as you're told,' my mother shouted.

'But she hates the water. She'll only cry.'

'Not if you're gentle with her. Let her dip her toes in the pools; coax her.'

I puckered my eyes against the glare of sun and sea, raised myself from the warm sand and stomped towards the lapping waves. Fionuala followed: full of endless chatter. The cool water trickled between my toes and suddenly I wanted to be with Aden and Sorcha. I looked longingly to where they were shouting and laughing, splashing and tumbling, spraying a thousand watery diamonds into the warm air. I ran towards them, the undertow dragging at my legs. I glanced back and saw Fionuala standing alone, a tiny dot by the water's edge. But I kept going. When I'd almost reached them I stood on tiptoe, jumped lightly into the air and executed a perfect ducky-dive. In the silent, green world I saw the outline of skinny limbs. I thrust myself forward, grabbed hold of a leg and pulled. I surfaced, and seconds later Aden emerged, coughing and spluttering.

'That wasn't funny, Aefe.'

'Grow up,' I snorted.

I glanced towards the shore and Fionuala was still where I'd left her. I dove once more and when I surfaced my brother and sister had moved away.

*

Theodore was very encouraging about the concept of my painting — a seascape in acrylics of Spanish Point at sunset and low tide. He offered to make another trip west when it was near completion. 'I know how useful a fresh gaze can be at that stage of the artistic endeavour,' he said, leaning over to pat my hand, 'so don't hesitate to call on me.'

The darkening sky is dotted with puffs of cloud that are lit from behind by the red glow of the evening sun. To the right of the canvas the shallows of low tide are a shimmering, crimson haze from which grey rocks erupt, stranded by the receding water.

Anxious to meet Theodore's deadline I'd spent the day working on the foreground and by evening exhausted, but satisfied with my progress, I cleaned my brushes, tidied the studio and, with whiskey in hand, returned to have one last look. I glanced over the rim of the tumbler and stopped dead. I started to shake, my teeth chattering against the glass.

*

The Silent Scream

I woke from a drunken sleep, dragged myself into the studio and walked round the canvas, eyes alert to danger. I scanned the foreground and again I began to tremble. Blood-red drops bubble in the shallow water. From the cluster of rocks a boulder looms, smooth and rounded, a curved figure with a mound of barnacles, clinging like an infant to its breast. The tiny creatures encrust the skull-like peak and cascade over the back of the boulder — an abundant wig of jet-black curls. As realization hit I started to search the canvas for other figures, but my nerve failed and I ran from the room.

*

I jumped into the Mini and drove through the twisting boreens, sending ducks and geese scattering in alarm. Screeching to a halt in Carrigaholt I cadged a boat from Sean Duggan and sailed through the Shannon Estuary and into the open sea.

As a strong westerly pitched and rolled the boat and lashed me with spray I remembered the story my father had told me about Sinann whose name had been given to the River Shannon. She'd touched the forbidden crystal fountain that protected the trees of knowledge and had unleashed a torrent of water that drowned her. Her corpse was carried downriver to the sea where my tiny craft was being tossed and buffeted.

In the distance angry waves flung themselves against the cliffs of Kerry. A small yacht passed to starboard and the young couple aboard waved and shouted their hellos. Shoals of fish parted in silvery swathes as the boat cleaved through the water. I saw again the strange figure in my painting and shut my eyes tightly to block it out.

A sudden gust swung the craft round and sent me sprawling. Soaked by the salty spray I was on my knees, clinging to the side, looking into the sea. Within inches of my horrified gaze, a face glowed eerily white and tendrils of hair floated like seaweed in the grey-green water. Pale blue eyes stared at me in mute appeal: a purple mouth opened in a silent scream.

Frantically, I clambered to my feet, brought the boat about and tacked for shore.

*

I leaned back to avoid the splashing of salt water; closed my eyes to avoid its sting. I ran my tongue in a circle round my lips and the briny taste was not unpleasant. My mother's voice, faint at first, was getting louder. It reached me across the wide expanse of sand.

'Where's Fionuala. Aefe, where is she?' she shouted.

The small body in the water was splashing and kicking, just below the surface. I stood still, paralysed, as the merciless heat of the sun beat like a hammer on my head. My mother's voice, full of fear and anger, was a great bell of sound.

'Where's your sister, where is she, Aefe?'

Sorcha was running through the water. She was closing in on me as Aden ran towards my mother.

The Silent Scream

Sorcha pushed my hand away, bent her knees, thrust her arms beneath the water, straightened up and Fionuala surfaced, rivulets streaming from her tiny frame. Her fine hair hung in silver threads; her eyes were wide and staring. My mother, coming from behind, shoved me aside and accepted Sorcha's offering of her youngest daughter.

She carried Fionuala out of the sea and lay her, face down, on the sand. Silent and afraid we circled her as she gently kneaded Fionuala's back. Fionuala coughed and water trickled from her mouth. She coughed again and water gushed onto the sand.

My mother lifted her and moulded her body to her breast in a protective hug. She walked back along the beach to where our clothes were. Rigid with anxiety Aden and Sorcha ran to keep up, careful not to look in my direction.

When my mother finished dressing Fionuala she turned towards me. Her glance rested on me for what seemed an eternity: her eyes cold and dark like the winter sea.

*

'I see you've decided to branch out,' Paddy 'The Slug' Griffin smiled knowingly, as he tucked into a bowl of Irish stew. He'd just delivered a handful of bills and I was in no mood to listen to his blather. 'I've been reading a book on the art, and if you don't mind me saying, missus, they say you should never mix the figurative with the landscape.' With the back of his hand he wiped a glob of greasy potato from his chin.

'And although I'm just a novice, I'd venture to say that the bould Theodore won't be much impressed with your latest creation.' Paddy slurped a spoonful of carrots and meat into his mouth. 'If you ask me,' he said, gleefully, 'a Madonna and Child rising out of a sea lappin' over red sand, looks too much like a watery version of the Slaughter of the Innocents to impress the Royal Academy.'

*

'I'll be driving down on Good Friday and staying at The Armada in Spanish Point for a couple of days. I think it's about time we talked things through. I'll see you then.' That was the letter from Fionuala that Paddy delivered two months previously. 'I'm coming too,' Sorcha had written.

*

I poured a generous measure of whiskey and, glass in hand, walked from the kitchen into the studio.

The evening was still. The wind, which had whipped the rolling waves into frothy foam early in the day, had died down. The last vestiges of spring light lingered like a child at bedtime.

I stood with my back to the window and studied the painting that rested on the easel. I would show the finished work to Fionuala and Sorcha when they arrived tomorrow. So let them come. It was long past time.

Gilded Shadows

Dreams of Salvation

A turf fire glows, casting an amber light into the darkness. Wisps of blue smoke swirl towards shadowy figures huddled round the blaze. The bulk of a man looms, his face crazed by the leaping flames, while a young girl leans forward, her golden hair sparkling in the flickering light. Her pointed face and ears quiver with malicious intent. Two children, hunched and expectant, cast a wary glance at the woman who sits in deep gloom, away from the fire. Stealthily, a shrouded figure slinks from the dark, waves lapping at its ankles and wet sand sucking at its feet. It plunges a knife towards the woman's back, but it doesn't reach her. Struggling against the rising tide and the thick mud the murky figure lunges again and again until, finally, metal hits bone. The woman's scream fills the pitch-black silence: a spurt of scarlet blood gushes from her mouth.

*

I woke, soaked in sweat, thrashing about like a landed fish. I rolled towards James' side of the bed, wanting his comforting warmth but his place was empty and cold and I remembered he was on nights. I took deep breaths and waited for the pounding of my heart to subside.

As the sullen light of dawn peeked through the curtains I fell asleep, untroubled at last by the nightmares which had started almost thirteen years before: after Mammy and I came back from Clare: the year I made my First Holy Communion.

The dreams had stopped when I left Ireland but now, a month after Mammy's sudden death, they were back again. And this time they were worse than ever.

*

'I'm going with Mammy and you're not,' I taunted my sisters and brother.

'Who wants to go to that godforsaken place?' Sorcha sneered.

'Shut up, Mammy's little pet,' said Aefe, with a toss of her abundant hair, 'or I'll hit you such a collop I'll send you spinning into the middle of next week. Anyway, for your information I'd rather be with Daddy.'

I don't think Aden heard me. He kept on reading his book and didn't try to kick me.

Mammy and I boarded the train at Kingsbridge Station. Daddy said, 'Be a good girl, Fionuala, and look after your mother.' He stood on the platform and as the train moved off he smiled and waved and mouthed words I couldn't hear. I hung out the window, waving until the train curled round a bend and he disappeared.

Dreams of Salvation

Mammy had made lots of sandwiches; egg for her and banana for me. She'd brought chocolate biscuits and lemonade that I didn't have to share with anyone. She talked about when she was a child: about growing up on the farm. 'I loved the spring,' she said, 'when the ewes licked the lambs clean, turning them into woolly bundles. Her eyes misted over with the pleasure of the memory. At the crack of dawn each morning she helped with the milking and went to the creamery with her older brother. She carried water from the well, churned butter, went to the bog to cut turf. Harvesting was her favourite time. 'Neighbours came from miles around to help save the hay. We boiled great pots of floury potatoes and cabbage over a roaring turf fire. Our finest goose was roasted in a griddle pan, its juices spiting and hissing and filling the air with its rich smell,' she remembered, her face girlish and joyful, only darkening when she talked of the killing of the pig. 'My favourite animals were the pigs,' she said. 'They followed me around like pet dogs. I sketched them with pencil and charcoal. Their large, roly-poly bodies, small heads, intelligent eyes and prominent snouts were easy to draw. I hated slaughter day. The pig man would come and tether the animal so he could stick him with the iron spike. I ran across the fields to escape, but it didn't matter how far I went I could still hear the screams when he drove the spike home,' she shuddered, her face dark with the memory.

But her eyes sparkled again as she told how she and her brothers and sisters, dozens of them it seemed to me, travelled to the hoolies held in all the houses of the district. 'Everyone would dance and sing', she smiled, 'and this is where young couples started their courting.' I wasn't sure what courting was, but I didn't want to ask and stop the flow of my mother's dazzling chatter.

*

I woke myself from my first nightmare by shrieking like a banshee. I sobbed and trembled so violently that Mammy sent for the doctor. He asked if I'd had any frightening experiences and Mammy frowned and said, 'No, not to my knowledge.' Daddy didn't say anything. He looked towards Mammy but she was focussing all her attention on me so he left the room. The doctor said to keep an eye on me but not to worry, as it wasn't uncommon for young girls to have violent dreams. He said I'd grow out of it.

After that my sisters refused to share a bedroom with me. As least Sorcha did — Aefe, seven years older than me, wasn't allowed. 'Aefe is growing beyond her strength so she needs uninterrupted sleep,' Mammy said, 'otherwise her legs won't be strong enough to hold her up and they'll buckle when she tries to walk. She needs her own room.'

Daddy opened his mouth to say something but changed his mind and walked away.

*

I hadn't been to Clare for four years — since I was three years old — and as the train raced towards the

Dreams of Salvation

West I tried to picture my grandparent's farm. I thought I remembered lots of green space enclosed by grey stone walls, huge mooing cows and a black and white dog that barked all the time, but I wasn't sure. Sorcha and Aden used to play 'Living in the Country' a lot and Sorcha would tell Aden to go across the big field and bring home the fat cows for milking before they burst, and to take that yapping dog with him, so maybe my memories were really theirs. I wondered why we didn't have family holidays anymore, why my sisters and brother weren't with us, but I didn't ask. I was afraid my questions would end my mother's happy mood.

*

'Pray, pray to the Blessed Virgin, and ask her to intercede with her holy son for you,' that's what Father Keane said when I first told him about the nightmares. 'With the blessing of the Holy Mother you'll find peace,' he said, his moon face gleaming with sweat. 'And sure you could give her a bit of a helping hand by turning your thoughts to joyful times.'

I stood outside the grey-stone terraced house on Rathmines Road. It was beside the canal and the foul smell of stagnant water hung heavy in the air. A statue of the Virgin Mary was displayed in the fanlight above the black, wooden door. The figure was, as always, draped in blue, her hands joined in prayer as she looked imploringly towards heaven.

It was a month after my first visit to Fr. Keane, two months short of my seventeenth birthday and I was about to act on another piece of his advice. 'Sure don't be always looking inward,' he'd said in his strong Kerry accent. 'Think of those worse off than yourself. Do some community-work. Join the Legion of Mary and help others, then you'll forget your own troubles.'

I pressed the bell once and a young man opened the door immediately. He was slim with deep-set, blue eyes and thick, black lashes — what Sorcha would call, 'A fine thing'. 'Well met by moonlight,' he said, his face breaking into a teasing smile. At my look of incomprehension he added, 'Don't mind my blather, I've just had my exam results and they're bloody great.'

'I've come for the Legion of Mary,' I said, wanting to be rid of him. His smile vanished and he nodded towards the dark interior.

'First floor, second door on the left.' He stood back and let me pass into the gloomy hall, then stepped out of the house and closed the door with a bang.

As soon as he'd gone I wanted him to come back and smile at me again.

*

We didn't have to change at Limerick Junction so Mammy was pleased. We only had to change at Ennis and then on to Milltown Malbay where Uncle Seamus, my mother's youngest brother, would meet us. Mammy always looked cross and stayed silent when Daddy sat by the fire reminiscing, but when she lay beside me after I woke, screaming and terrified from the horror of my nightmares, just the two of us together in the dim nightlight, she told me about her childhood exploits with Seamus.

Once a year, with great fanfare, the travelling cinema arrived in Milltown Malbay for a stay of two nights and my Granda took them into town in the ass and cart and left them with their Auntie Bridie and Uncle P.J. so that they could see both films. Mammy's favourite film was Stagecoach with John Wayne. Crammed into the tiny community hall, sitting on hard wooden forms, licking frantically at sugary lollipops, they looked in wonder as the Ringo Kid outwitted all the baddies. 'We thought it was wonderful,' Mammy said, speaking softly and stroking my hair. 'The stagecoach swayed like a drunk across the hazy, flickering screen, and the horses were spurred to ever-greater efforts trying to outrun the galloping bandits and Indians,' she laughed quietly at the memory.

'On our next trip to collect turf from the bog, Seamus and I lashed the poor horse into a frenzy and sped down the low road shouting, 'Yaa hah, Yaa hah, giddiup ya ornery critter!'

Unfortunately, Joe Breen told on them and their Da said they had to go to bed without tea for two nights. 'But my mother thought a whipping like the one we'd inflicted on the horse was a more fitting punishment,' Mammy said, without bitterness. So they were sent to their parents' bedroom where a reluctant Granda was handed the reins and left to get on with it. On cue, Mammy and Seamus howled in unison as their father whacked the feather bed with all his might.

GILDED SHADOWS

Father Keane's remedy for my nightly torment wasn't working. I was out of happy memories and, although I attended the weekly meetings, prayed fervently with the other members of our presidium and tried to concentrate on the hardships endured by the elderly on whom we lavished our good works, the terrible dreams still plagued me. To make matters worse the lingering foul smell of the filthy homes we cleaned for the needy made me want to vomit every time I looked at food.

Two months passed before I admitted to myself that it wasn't for the love of God and his Blessed Mother, or for the good of those less fortunate than myself that I continued to visit the house on Rathmines Road.

'All that praying is wearing you out, you're as pale as a ghost,' the young man with the blue eyes said, opening the door as I mounted the steps, 'or maybe you've been pining for me,' he grinned.

'I'm not feeling the best,' I murmured, reluctant to meet his impish gaze.

'Leave it to Dr. Lawlor,' he said, and shut the door behind him with a resounding bang. Taking my elbow he led me down the steps, along the road, past the church of Our Lady of Refuge to the Rathmines Inn where he guided me to a seat in a quiet corner, headed for the bar and returned sipping beer. He handed me a glass of wine. 'Red wine is good for the constitution,' he said. 'Take it from one who knows absolutely nothing, but who never lets that stand in the way of giving advice on absolutely everything. It's good practice for when I qualify,' he laughed.

I didn't tell him I was a Pioneer; that I'd never had an alcoholic drink; that I was too young to be in a pub. I met his smiling gaze without flinching, and took my first sip.

*

The train finally stopped at the tiny station of Milltown Malbay, the most westerly station in the county. 'Sure if it went any further you'd end up in the Atlantic and be borne on its mighty waves to New York or Boston,' my Uncle Seamus said with a poetic flourish.

My uncle had come to meet us in the pony and trap. The wood of the bevelled carriage, smooth and darkened with age, shone in the evening sunlight and Dubh the pony munched on the grassy verge. When we left the streets of the small town behind Seamus allowed Dubh his head, and the pony trotted along the narrow boreens, weaving from side to side to avoid potholes, stones and the hens and ducks that strayed into his path.

*

James Lawlor was his name and he came from Carlow. He wanted to be a doctor and was waiting to hear which medical school would accept him. My heart sank when he said he couldn't wait to leave Ireland and had applied to Leeds and Birmingham. His parents were paying rent on his tiny room in Rathmines to give him access to the National Library where he could study every day. A fan of Joyce, he opted instead to wander in the footsteps of Leopold Bloom, a copy of *Ulysses* clutched to his admiring breast. He invited me to join him on his literary rambles and we arranged to take a bus to Sandycove to gaze at the Martello Tower.

As I looked into his roguish eyes I bade a silent farewell to the Legion of Mary.

*

My grandmother waited like a bird of prey at the doorway of the whitewashed cottage in Cloonlaheen. She was dressed entirely in black: her iron-grey hair pulled back into a tight bun: her nose hooked and dangerous. Above her the thatched roof had faded from the buttery yellow of its early days to a grey that matched her hair. Frantic hens strutted among us, pecking viciously at the black earth. Away to my right a posse of geese stood, erect and challenging, ready to pounce. Aunts and uncles milled round, cousins came running from the haggart.

We crowded into the dark interior of the cottage, our feet ringing on the flagstones. To the left, a turf-fire burned orange and yellow in the open hearth, sending out its primitive smell of earth and roots. A black, iron kettle, suspended from a chain, started to boil. On the right, against the wall, a mirror glowed in the dancing light. I glanced towards it and saw Mammy's pale face surrounded by leaping flames. I grabbed hold of her hand and didn't let go.

*

Dreams of Salvation

A grey mist crept in from the sea as the mail boat eased its bulk away from Dún Laoghaire Pier. I waved to James as he leaned over the side, shouting his goodbyes that were lost in the din of departure. Tears streamed down my face as the vessel headed out to sea. The ship had disappeared into the night, but I still stood, gripping the cold railings, frightened to let go in case my legs gave way.

'I think it's time you went home now, miss.' The voice was gruff and hoarse. 'It doesn't do for young ladies to hang about the pier at this time of night.'

I smiled wanly at the porter and headed towards the bus stop.

*

James' letters were full of the exhilaration of living in a strange city, away from what he called, 'The stifling narrow-mindedness of Ireland'. His training was demanding and exhausting but he loved it: 'The challenge, the freedom, the newness of it all.'

On his brief visits home we retraced our literary rambles and he talked about the future, his eyes bright with excitement. He wanted me to join him in England and then later, when he qualified, we could travel the world together, maybe even work in Africa.

His plans frightened me. I knew even if I summoned the courage to follow him, Mammy and Daddy would never allow me to go to Birmingham. 'The cursed English are responsible for all the sorry woes of Ireland,' I'd heard Daddy say, over and over again, as we sat round the fire on a winter's evening, 'and no child of mine will ever set foot in that godforsaken place.' Mammy remained silent, but she nodded her head in agreement and none of us dared demur.

*

'You take her home.' I said to Aden. I'll do the first stint of the vigil. You can come back later.' Aden put a supporting hand under Mammy's elbow and led her out of the church towards the waiting car.

I walked quickly towards the side chapel where, minutes before, the priest had prayed over my father's coffin.

The church was quiet and dimly lit and shadows played on the high walls and ceiling. Statues loomed out of the dark and I bit my lip to prevent myself from crying out.

I pushed the heavy door of the chapel open and stopped suddenly. Daddy's coffin was raised on a metal stand. In the dim interior, candles flickered and blinked, sending wavering shapes round and round the room. A figure was draped over the casket, arms outstretched, face pressed against the smooth wood. A few seconds passed before I recognized my sister Aefe. As I stood, unsure what to do, her shoulders rose and fell and her rasping sobs filled the eerie space.

The heavy door slipped from my grasp and I walked quietly away.

*

Dreams of Salvation

A week after Daddy's funeral I told Mammy that I was leaving Dublin. I knew I'd been her favourite: that she'd spoilt and indulged me: lavished her love on me and had little left over for Aefe, Aden and Sorcha. I wanted to tell her I would stay, that I would never leave her, that I'd be the daughter who'd always look after her, but I knew I couldn't.

When the time came to say good-bye I stood, mute and forlorn, as my act of betrayal caused her handsome face to fold and collapse. Unable to bear the treacherous silence, Mammy turned and left the room. She hesitated at the door and looked at me with ravenous eyes, as though she knew she was seeing me for the last time.

*

Mammy glowed with delight at being back in the wild countryside of her childhood. She tackled the work with gusto, carrying turf from the haggart to the house, digging vegetables for dinner, herding the cows, thrilling to the pleasure of being outdoors. Her spirit, stifled by the city, expanded to fill the wide, green space on the westerly edge of Ireland. I watched as, time and again, she stood and gazed at the scattered cottages strung out across the marshy, stony fields and the gentle, ancient hills. In the evenings, when the work was finished, she sat on a boulder outside the cottage and sketched the peaceful scene.

To amuse me while she worked she handed me a wooden box filled with torn comics, a pack of cards with all the Hearts missing, dozens of pieces of jigsaw puzzle without the picture and, at the bottom of the box, a book called The Myths and Legends of Ireland. On the cover, a beautiful, red-haired maiden sits gazing towards the glow of a fire which burns in the distance. Small, demonic figures circle the blaze in a manic dance, their pointed faces agleam with malice.

I opened the book and on the flyleaf, in my sister's bold handwriting was written, 'This book belongs to Aefe De Danann, aged ten. If you read it without asking me you will be cursed.'

*

I loved that Birmingham was slap, bang in the middle of the country, miles from the sea, with no stinking river cutting it in half. 'We've got more canals than Venice,' James said, laying claim to the strange place.

I visualized the city as a gigantic circle: a perfect whole criss-crossed by a system of connecting roads, canals and streams. I arrived just in time to see the full glory of the flowering trees that festooned the suburbs with masses of pink and white blossom.

Mammy hadn't asked about my living arrangements. She was afraid she'd get the same answer Aefe had given her when she went to live in sin with Paul O'Brien and Mammy said she'd, 'scandalized the entire city by her lewd behaviour.' Thankfully, the two students who lived with James in a tiny terraced house in Selly Oak were ignorant of Dublin sensibilities and were unfazed by the fact that I was sharing James' room.

Dreams of Salvation

Being away from home made me giddy with fear and excitement. But I loved it all. I had James, and for a short while it felt good.

*

Mammy was digging in the plot so I ran with the forbidden book to the back of the cottage, to my secret place behind the rick of turf. Hidden from view I opened the pages and read how Aislinn, trapped on the floor of her valley after the great flood, used the magical powers learnt from her mother to make a huge bubble in which she could survive for a day and night. All around her the water rose and the faces of her neighbours and friends, ugly with terror, brushed against the watery wall, looking at her with staring eyes and open mouths.

Although there were words I didn't understand, the drawings of Aislinn and the terrifying images of the people outside her safe bubble scared me and made the hairs on the back of my neck prickle. But I kept on reading.

*

For almost a year, curled each night against James' warm body the nightmares had stopped, but when Mammy died, suddenly and alone thirteen months after Daddy, it all began again. This time there was a new horror. I recognized the figure that stabs the woman huddled in the dark, the woman who gurgles and chokes as a spurt of scarlet blood gushes from her mouth. At last I knew who it was, and the knowledge was too much to bear.

I longed for my mother, called out for her in the night. I couldn't believe I would never see her again, that I'd never feel her comforting hands as they stroked my hair, hear her voice as she lay beside me in the dark.

The memory of her piercing glance as she turned back to look at me one last time before I left for England, a glance that contained all the love and sorrow of a lifetime, clawed at my heart.

'You must let me get the treatment you need, Fionuala.' James tried hard to keep the panic from his voice. 'I'm not qualified to deal with this. You need expert help.'

But I didn't want to talk to a stranger in a strange country about my dreams. I'd learnt that the Irish were hated in Birmingham and I thought the doctors would think I was evil, or maybe mad: that they'd have me put away: that I might never see Ireland again.

In the end the matter was out of my hands, and the hospital arranged for me to see Dr. Taylor.

*

I heard footsteps close-by and jumped quickly to my feet and ran to the nearby field, stuffing the precious book up my gansey. The ground was marshy and I leapt wildly from hummock to hummock. I stumbled and my foot was sucked into the boggy earth. I lunged at the dry-stone wall and grabbed at clumps of delicate pink flowers that came away in my hand. My frantic movement dislodged one of the higgledy-piggledy stones and its sharp edge scraped the skin off my leg as it fell and sank slowly into the mire. I hauled myself over the wall and jumped onto the firm ground of the next field.

*

Every two weeks I took the bus to Moseley and there, in a dingy consulting room in Uffculme Clinic, Dr. Taylor and I trawled my brief history, searching for the clue that might free me from the past. 'Tell me about your family,' she said, 'anything that comes to mind, anything at all.'

I told her about Daddy and Aefe: how they were always together: how in all my childhood memories Aefe stands next to Daddy, talking and listening by turns, the two of them engrossed in each other, oblivious to everyone else. I told her how Aden and Sorcha only allowed me to breach their private world if Aefe was not around. How Daddy was always watchful of Mammy's moods. How Aefe pinched and kicked me when no one else was looking. I told her about my dreams.

But most of the time with Dr. Taylor was spent unravelling my memories of the holiday I'd spent with Mammy in Clare, without Daddy and my sisters and brother, just the two of us together.

*

I sat with my back to the wall and opened the book once again. Aislinn knew she was trapped: there was no escape from the dark, deep water. Greedily, I scanned the pages. As Aislinn lay in terror in the darkness, snippets of old nightmares came back to haunt her, until she was beset by the worst nightmare of all. Slowly, her lithe, young body changed shape: she sprouted a scaly fishtail, webbed fingers and gills. The image filled her with horror and as I looked at the drawing of the half-woman half-fish I was horrified too. But Aislinn forced herself to use the gift of her mother's spells to take on the shape she dreaded most so that she could pierce the wall of water and swim for the surface.

*

Ten months after my first appointment at Uffculme Clinic, the day I'd been dreading arrived. It was my last visit: from here on I was on my own. 'I think we've achieved everything possible from these sessions,' Dr. Taylor said as she dragged her gaze from the branches of the oak that tapped an intermittent rhythm on the window. She swivelled her chair and faced me. Her mouth twitched into a faint smile and her eyes were gentle and kind as she said, 'The time has come, Fionuala, to confront the demon.'

*

On my way home on the crowded bus I thought again about the story I'd read all those years ago. Aislinn had escaped her terrible fate by changing herself into the image she most feared, into her worst nightmare. My worst nightmare was my own image, committing a heinous act. To find peace I needed to understand why my sleeping self emerged nightly from the gloom and plunged a knife into the back of the woman who sat in the shadows.

*

'What did your sister do to you?' The soft voice was carried to me on the wind. I sat still, afraid to move. I heard it again. 'What did your sister do to you?' It came from behind, from where the sun had begun to set. I imagined the little people of my grandmother's stories who preyed on unloved children. I thought of Aefe's curse. Something cold touched my bare neck and I screamed.

'Jesus, you Jackeens are very jittery. Sure I only asked you a question.' I turned and saw my cousin Dermot standing on the perilous wall.

'How did you get here?' I asked, my voice barely a whisper.

'Wasn't I sent from the house? You're wanted for your tea. Give us your hand and I'll pull you up. It's easier to walk on the wall than through the field.'

I followed him carefully along the jagged wall, fearful of the eager land on either side. When we reached the haggart Dermot jumped onto firm ground and waited for me to join him.

*

'It's not uncommon to suppress the memory of a frightening experience, Fionuala,' Dr, Taylor had told me. 'The details of the incident can lie buried for years. It might never be retrieved and the patient can live without trauma, ignorant of the fact that anything is amiss. But your nightmares were the signal that something was wrong and the death of your mother precipitated a crisis, creating the conditions that made recovery possible.'

At the mention of my mother I started to cry, but as I wiped away the tears Dr. Taylor's voice was quiet and reassuring. 'We know such crises are not without risk Fionuala,' she said, 'but with support and help the patient can confront their fears, deal with them, and go on to enjoy a more tranquil life.'

*

Dermot offered me his hand to help me from the wall and he asked once again. 'What did your sister do to you?'

'I have two sisters, I said, trying not to cry.'

'Your eldest sister — Aefe. I heard your Mammy tell my Mammy that Aefe did something terrible to you.'

I knew this couldn't be true. Mammy didn't know about the spiteful pinches and sneaky kicks which Aefe inflicted: she didn't see her do it and I was too scared of my sister to tell.

'Aefe tried to kill you,' Dermot said, his eyes shining with excitement.

'You're telling lies,' I said and ran to find my mother. His voice followed me. 'Your sister tried to kill you,' he jeered.

*

Dreams of Salvation

With Dr. Taylor's help I'd remembered what Dermot had told me, with such glee, all those years before, and had started to untangle the web of my dreams.

Even in sleep I was too frightened to attack my real adversary, the person I most feared. Instead, coward that I am, I directed my anger at the woman I'd loved most in the world and who'd loved me in return, the woman I'd abandoned and whom I would never see again.

Dr. Taylor confirmed what I'd dreaded most. Heartsick and frightened, I knew I'd have to look to Aefe, my sister with the auburn hair and slanting, green eyes, for salvation. I had to find out if what Dermot said was true and, if it was, why she would want to do such a thing.

During the months I visited Dr. Taylor I realized that great swathes of the past are lost to us, not simply because we can't recall what happened, but also because we contrive to forget what we dare not remember.

*

I knew that all the counselling in the world couldn't give me the courage to confront Aefe alone. For that I would need help, and with Mammy and Daddy dead and Aden away on his travels, my only hope was Sorcha.

But Aefe was not the only sister who didn't like me. Sorcha had called me 'a sanctimonious cow,' on more than one occasion. As far as she was concerned I still belonged to the Legion of Mary and I knew she had no time for the church, would have abandoned it completely if it hadn't been for Mick. 'A crowd of bloody hypocrites, that's what they all are — bishops, priests, nuns, the whole scalding lot of them,' she was fond of saying.

On my visits home I hadn't endeared myself to her. In fact, I'd set out to annoy her by deliberately playing the 'Holy Mary' act for all it was worth. (I had to get my own back on someone and she'd always been the easiest target).

But I needed Sorcha. She'd managed better than the rest of us to get her life together, so I would write to her and ask for her help and hope she wouldn't let me down.

Gilded Shadows

Ashes to Ashes

A Year after Da died Ma joined him. Without his calming presence the fierce anger that had burned below the surface throughout our childhood flared up and consumed her. Alone and furious she suffered a massive heart attack.

Her funeral was a nightmare. The rain lashed down on the fresh sods, releasing a sour, earthy smell. A handful of mourners stood huddled round the grave in Mount Jerome Cemetery and sank slowly into the mud. Ma's brothers and sisters couldn't leave their farms, Aden couldn't leave his ship, so it was left to Aefe, Fionuala, myself — heavily pregnant with Joseph — and a dusting of neighbours to do the honours.

'Sure the poor thing died of a broken heart,' lamented Biddy O'Driscoll, tears welling in her red-rimmed eyes. 'She just couldn't bear to stay in this world without him.'

'They were a perfect match; that's what they were; a rare couple,' sobbed Kathleen Roche, wisps of grey hair plastered to her face in the driving rain.

'I'd rather join Ma than listen to much more of this,' I whispered to Fionuala who looked at me in wide-eyed horror before collapsing in a heap, sobbing and bawling. 'Feck the pregnancy,' I said, 'I'm having a drink, a large one.'

'Sorcha doesn't mean to be brutal,' said Biddy, as she tried to drag Fionuala out of the muck. 'Sure she's just overcome with grief, although grief or not she shouldn't be drinking in her condition.'

I drew back my hand and was about to land her one on her fat, blabbering gob when Aefe stepped between us and took the slap instead.

'Can't cope without dear old Aden?' Aefe raised a quizzical eyebrow, as she dabbed at the drop of blood on her lip.

'Have you two lost your minds?' wailed Fionuala. You're a disgrace! I want James. I need James.'

'Well, piss off back to Birmingham to your poxy James. He's welcome to you,' I roared.

'That's exactly what I'm going to do,' she sobbed. 'Now that Mammy and Daddy are gone I'll never set foot in this godforsaken country again.'

With a great effort I calmed my raging hormones. 'But we're expecting you home when the baby arrives,' I simpered. 'We want you to be godmother.'

Fionuala snivelled into her hankie. 'That's the first I've heard of it.'

'We were going to tell you after the funeral. We wanted it to be a surprise.'

Ashes to Ashes

She dabbed at her eyes. 'I don't suppose I can refuse. There's little doubt that the child will need spiritual guidance.'

I was sorely tempted to slap her on the gob as well, but I'd almost ruined my carefully laid plans once that day. I needed Fionuala to make regular trips to Dublin: my sanity depended on it.

*

Three days after Ma's funeral Fionuala started blathering on about the past. 'Leave me out of it,' I remember saying as we strolled along Sandymount strand. 'Just leave me out of it. Ma and Da are dead so there's no point in raking over the family ashes.'

The tide was far out and a salty whiff rose from clumps of seaweed scattered over the vast expanse of sand. The cries of children mingled with the shrill call of the gulls that soared and swooped, searching for morsels left by the tide. A young man, his long, black hair floating in the wind, was digging for bait.

In the crimson haze of the lowering sun I visualized my Da, bent over his spade. Aefe was, as always, standing next to him, her lips moving silently, her words carried away on the breeze. Aden chased me, round and round in circles. My Ma sat alone among the bundles of clothes and shoes, looking into the distance.

Fionuala droned on. 'That's my point,' she said, 'now they're no longer here we can talk to Aefe without upsetting them.'

And then she fecked off back to Birmingham.

GILDED SHADOWS

It was 1977 and there were great goings-on over the water. It was Lizzie's jubilee and everyone was getting hysterical about the possibility that Virginia Wade might actually win Wimbledon. Fionuala, my little sassenach sister, had tickets for the women's finals and couldn't wait to leave Dublin.

'It's just as well Ma had the tact to die when she did,' I said to Mick, 'otherwise Fionuala would have had to cancel her trip to sassenach heaven.'

Mick lowered the newspaper and looked at me in that annoying, deadpan way he has. 'Pregnancy doesn't bring out the best in you, sweetheart,' he said, and quickly raised the paper as I flung a wet dishcloth in his direction.

*

I've never been one for looking back. There's enough torment in the present without digging for it in the past. Well, there was two and a half years ago when Fionuala started on about uncovering the family secret that, according to her, had blighted our lives: Ma and Da were dead and I was young — too young to be pregnant on my fourth in five years. I'd been desperate enough to try gin and a hot bath on the third but it hadn't worked. And I still couldn't keep my hands off Mick. His powerful physique and the way his dark hair curled against the nape of his neck made my stomach flip every time I looked at him. I wondered if I was normal and, although Fionuala is my kid sister by five years, I mentioned it to her. The prissy little cow nearly had a stroke. It was all right for her. She knew nothing about the tortures of coitus interruptus when the job had to be finished manually. She was living in a place where sex was on tap, without the worry, morning, noon and night. But she swore on a stack of bibles that she would never use anything. 'The church forbids sex outside marriage,' she said.

'You're not trying to tell me you and James have never done it!'

'James and I don't discuss our private life,' she said. 'But if you must know we've opted for celibacy. Of course you need willpower. You can't indulge your every whim. You have to mortify your body to save your soul.'

'Bollocks,' I said. You don't see many of the clergy mortifying their bodies. They live in the height of comfort; their every need attended to.'

'They live celibate lives. They take vows, renouncing the pleasures of the flesh.'

'My arse,' I said. Their housekeepers are not there just to feed and water them.'

'May God forgive you, Sorcha O'Sullivan!' Her face went scarlet and her baby-blue eyes stood out on sticks. It's easy to get a rise out of Fionuala. But when she spewed all that rubbish about 'confronting Aefe with the reality of the past so that we could explore our shared history and put our ghosts to rest once and for all,' I wondered about her sanity. I mean where does she get that shite from? If that's the way they talk over the water it's no wonder the ones who emigrate go queer in the head.

But the silly cow had started something. In quiet moments, when I was feeding the baby, or when the kids were, by some miracle, all asleep, wisps of memories floated, unbidden, to the surface.

*

I was five years old and Aden, who was six, had talked his friends into letting me play. I'd been captured and was in the den. Paddy Murphy was on guard but Aden slipped past him, touched my outstretched hand and shouted 'relievio' and I flew like the wind.

We went indoors out of the blistering sun for a drink of water. My brother ran along the cold, gloomy hall towards the kitchen and I chased after him. The tangy smell of stewing rhubarb drifted in the air as Aden pushed open the kitchen door and came to a sudden halt. Thousands of dust motes swirled, like swarming insects, in the beam of light that escaped from the sun-filled room. Unable to stop myself I bumped into him, but he stood his ground.

I looked round him and saw Ma sitting awkwardly at the kitchen table, her enormous belly squashed beneath its scratched surface. A torch of sunlight, streaming through the window, turned the copper tints in her hair into golden sparks. Her shoulders rose and fell rhythmically, and then a great sob escaped her swollen body.

I opened my mouth to say her name but Aden stopped me with a look. He took my hand and pulled me, quietly, back into the shadows of the hall.

Ashes to Ashes

Sean squealed in delicious fright as Mick chased him round and round the garden. Mary, unable to catch them, jumped up and down on the spot, adding her shrieks to the rumpus. Elaine, unsure whether to laugh or cry, clutched the handle of the go-car where Joseph slept and sucked her thumb. Mick grabbed Sean by the waist, threw him in the air; caught him as he plummeted towards the lawn. And then the girls were clinging to Mick's legs laughing and screaming in delight.

I unpegged the tiny garments from the clothesline and put them into the basket. Heading for the house I glanced back at Mick and the kids and thought about my own sisters and brother: how the shock of my father's death had scattered them like shot from a gun. The poor man was hardly in the ground before Aefe made a dash from Dublin to Clare. Aden buggered off and joined the merchant navy, fulfilling what he called a long-held and, until that time strangely secret ambition, to sail the seven seas. Fionuala showed no inclination to hang around the mother who'd spoiled her rotten. She took herself off on the mail boat to Holyhead where she caught a train, changed at Crewe and joined James Lawlor (medical student) in Birmingham. I was the only one left in Dublin.

'O.k. kids, time for tea,' Mick's voice floated on the evening air, breathless and full of laughter. As I folded the washed clothes ready for ironing, I licked the salt water from my lips and, quickly, before Mick could see, buried my face in one of Joseph's freshly laundered nappies.

*

You can't really blame Fionuala, revelling in the past is a national sport: they give medals for it. My Da's greatest pleasure was to sit at a roaring fire on a dark winter's evening, sip a glass of porter, and regale us with stories. Most of the tales were about Ireland's fight for freedom: Father Murphy and the boys of Wexford who'd taken on the mighty British and suffered a glorious defeat; young Robert Emmet's failed rebellion and courageous death; the heroes of the Easter Rising in 1916 who knew they couldn't win, but decided to fight because their cause was just. 'We must never forget the past,' he would say, staring into the fire as though hypnotized by the dancing flames. 'Sure if we don't learn the lessons of the past we're all doomed.' If he was flutered, he'd burst into song, *Boolavogue, Bold Robert Emmet, A Nation Once Again,* and we'd sing along, our tinny warbling drowned by his powerful bass.

*

'Give it back! Give it to your brother, Mary, this minute. Now!' I said. Mary clung to the little engine with all her might, resisting Sean's attempts to pull it from her. It was Sunday morning and Mick had nipped for a pint after mass with his brother Joe, and I was peeling potatoes when Mary mounted yet another raid on Sean's precious train set. She ignored my entreaties:

her lower lip a shelf of determination. I wiped my hands and, kneeling in front of her, prised the engine from her closed fist.

'I want my Daddy', she wailed, I want my Daddy.'

'Your Daddy's not here,' I said, returning to the sink, 'so be a good girl and play with your own toys.' I turned on the tap and the gurgle of water blotted out the whizzing of the doll's pram as it hurtled towards me and caught me a painful blow that buckled my knees. As I scrambled to my feet Mary screwed up her face and opened her mouth like a yawning baby-hippo.

'I want my Daddy, I want my Daddy,' she screamed.

*

I was seven years old and I stood sucking my thumb, eyes lowered, scared to look at my big sister whose skinny frame was rigid with determination as she squared up to Ma.

'I want to go with Daddy.' Aefe's voice was sulky and I glanced in panic from her to my mother. She stared at Ma's angry face, her green eyes round and hard like the pebbles she kicked towards the crashing waves. The smell of brine hung heavy in the air and the light of the sun turned her copper-red hair into a fiery crown.

'No, you can look after Fionuala while I walk along the beach,' Ma insisted.

'Let her help me fish Deirdre,' my Da coaxed. 'Sure can't Aden and Sorcha take care of their little sister?'

GILDED SHADOWS

With an insolent swagger Aefe followed my Da along Killiney strand. From a safe distance she glanced back, her face ablaze with triumph.

*

Unwittingly, Fionuala was my salvation. After Joseph was born I still fancied Mick like mad but he was as bad as Fionuala when it came to contraception.

It was seven years since women's libbers went up the North, bought contraceptives and declared them to the custom officers when they came back to the Republic so as to embarrass the government into changing the law, but dinosaur Mick still referred to them as, 'a crowd of shameless hussies with no respect for themselves or the church.'

You couldn't mention poor Mary McGee's name in front of him. Her contraceptives were confiscated at customs and she took the government to court to challenge them for breaching her constitutional rights and she had most of the women (and men) in the country cheering her on. Not my Mick. Oh, no. As far as he was concerned she was the 'Whore of Babylon'.

The doctor would have prescribed condoms but Mick wasn't having any. The pope said 'NO', and that was good enough for him, the big sap. They'd had the swinging sixties in London and ten years later omodons like Mick were still stuck in the dark ages in Dublin. If he wasn't so gorgeous I'd have left him.

We tried the rhythm method which meant having sex about three friggin' times a month. I was climbing the walls. Actually I was chasing Mick all over the house but he didn't want to know. Well he did, but he said someone in the family had to show restraint so he barricaded himself in the box room. The kids heard me banging on the door and tumbled from their beds to join the game of hide and seek. Sean frightened himself by saying the bogeyman had captured his Daddy and he started to cry. Not to be outdone Mary sent up a deafening howl; alone and scared in her cot Elaine joined in the terrifying chorus. Mercifully, Joseph slept through it all.

But Mick, the bastard, stayed behind the locked door.

*

I couldn't take anymore so I was off to England on the mail boat to get a year's supply (on the pretext of visiting Fionuala) when the woman herself came to the rescue.

I was about to put the kids to bed and say goodbye when she arrived on one of her surprise visits from Birmingham (landing me in it with Mick). In she comes, and before a hello or how are you? she asks, 'Am I in time for the family rosary?'

'Mammy, what's the family rosary?' pipes Sean, before I can shove him into the hall and upstairs to bed.

'I hope you're not neglecting their religious education, Sorcha. A Catholic mother has a responsibility to make sure that the home is a place of worship.' Fionuala's eyes gleamed with fervour. Not for the first time I wondered if she had a drink problem.

And anyway it was all a bit rich coming from her. She wasn't fooling me with her malarkey about the family rosary and celibacy. I was certain sure that she and James were living in sin in Birmingham and that they were at it like rabbits. No man with eyes like James Lawlor would live a celibate life — I'd stake my babies' lives on it.

'I don't suppose James sent a package for me?' I ventured.

'As a matter of fact he sent some medication for the kids. Apparently they'll be needing a regular supply.'

So I didn't leave for England after all. James had come up trumps. I'd cornered him at Joseph's christening, putting my carefully hatched plan into operation, terrified he wouldn't agree.

'Sure thing,' he said.

'You understand,' I said, Fionuala mustn't know what's in the packages.'

'Fionuala wouldn't know if she was carrying a red-hot poker,' he said, 'so you've no worry on that score.'

Fionuala had come to Joseph's christening as the Virgin Mary, all got up in blue organza with a white mantilla draped over her blonde hair.

'She thinks it's a friggin' fancy dress', I whispered to Mick.

Anyway, after the splashing of the water and the crossing of the palm with silver (the priest's that is) and the hundred and one photographs Fionuala insisted on taking, she sidled up to me and continued the campaign she'd started a few months before, just after Ma died.

'I told you we're losing Aefe,' she said. 'She hasn't even bothered to come to the christening.'

'She's too busy,' I said. She's got an important commission, besides I'm not sure we ever had Aefe. I'm not sure we ever really wanted her.'

'Exactly, that's exactly what I mean. But it's time we rediscovered our sister.'

'That won't be difficult,' I said. Take the Galway Road out of Dublin and when you can go no further turn left and into Clare.'

Fionuala gave me a withering look and moved away to have one last word with Father Connor.

*

My Ma disagreed with my Da about the wisdom of looking back. 'No good ever came from digging round in the past,' was her response to his historical meanderings. As he warmed to his subject she would flash him a flinty look, avert her eyes and gaze into the embers of the fire. We children knew, instinctively, that it wasn't Ireland's past she was referring to.

So maybe Fionuala's need to uncover the past was born of my Ma's desire to bury it. She was convinced, poor eejit, that if she discovered Ma's secret we could return to a mythical time of familial bliss — that Aefe, herself and me (and Aden when he was around) would be great pals, that we'd be living off the pig's back.

But I'm with my Ma on this. Leave well alone. Sure you might as well attempt to plait fog as try to unravel the past.

*

'What are these?'

'Do you think I've got eyes in the back of my head,' I said. I was bent double over the bath trying to keep Joseph afloat and couldn't see what Mick held in his hand.

'Get up off your knees and answer me,' Mick's voice was thick with anger.

'What ails you?' I turned my head and glimpsed a strip of silver foil in his outstretched hand. I lifted Joseph from the water, grabbed a towel and pushed past Mick. He followed me into the bedroom. 'Answer me,' he said, his voice getting louder.

'You know what they are,' I said, 'only you didn't want me to tell you. You wanted to believe we weren't getting pregnant because of the grace of god.'

'You had no right.' he shouted and ran downstairs. 'You had no right,' he shouted again, as he banged the front door.

*

'Do you realize what you are saying, Deirdre?' my Da's voice was loud and shaking with anger.

'Keep you voice down,' my mother hissed. 'You'll wake the children.'

'Do you know what you're accusing your daughter of?' my father insisted.

'I tell you she held her under. I saw it with my own eyes. She's evil, I tell you and it's your fault. You turned her funny with all those stories about myths and magic. You should never have given her that book. But there's no use talking to you. Sure you won't hear a word said against her.'

'You need help, Deirdre,' Da said, quieter now. 'You need help. I know you never wanted her. Jesus, didn't you throw yourself down the stairs trying to get rid of her, but this is going too far. Surely to God you can't hate her that much?'

'It wasn't Aefe I didn't want. I didn't want any child. I wanted time to paint. I wanted to find out how good I was.' My Ma spat the words at my Da.

There was a long silence. 'But you might have killed yourself. Sure I might have lost both of you.' My father's voice was soft and weary.

Sucking on my aching tooth I tiptoed away from the kitchen door and crept back to bed.

*

After weeks of drenching rain the weather cleared. 'Let's go to Seapoint on Sunday,' said Mick, smiling broadly, pleased with his brilliant idea.

'I'm not taking four children *and* a go-car *and* a picnic on a bus,' I said, closing the wardrobe door with a bang.

'No need to sweetheart, I'll borrow the van from work and ask Joe, Aine and the kids to come too.

It was a perfect day for an outing to the sea, hot and sunny with a light breeze. The food that Aine and

I had spread on a rug, although liberally sprinkled with sand, had been devoured. Mick, Jo and the older kids were playing in the shallows and the babies were asleep. I lay on the warm sand and listened to the shouts and laughter of the children as they splashed in the water. The warmth of the sun and the gentle lapping of the waves lulled me to the brink of sleep and then I was jerked awake by the note of alarm in Aine's voice. 'Joe', she shouted, 'Joe, get Patrick, he's too far out, he's too far out.'

*

Aden and I were jumping and diving, jumping and diving in the cool, green sea. Each time we surfaced we coughed and laughed, choking on the salty water. Across the expanse of sea and sand a voice was raised in panic. Aden responded more quickly than me. He headed towards the shore, at first running then swimming, then running again, struggling against the drag of the waves.

'It's Ma', he shouted over his shoulder, 'there's something wrong with Ma.'

Ma was running towards Aefe who was standing in the sea, water lapping her waist. As Ma ran she shouted, her voice shrill with fright. Aden headed for Ma and I veered towards my older sister.

Aefe stood, slightly bent, her hands beneath the foaming water. A tiny foot broke the surface and horror almost stopped me in my tracks, but I lunged forward and pushed my big sister's arm with all my might, knocking her off balance. Fionuala's pale body kicked and splashed its way to the top.

*

It was one of those summer evenings sent to remind us that autumn lurks in the shadows. The bright day gave way to deep gloom as fog descended and the air turned damp and cold. Indoors the house was cosy and quiet, the children asleep. I tiptoed into their bedrooms, kissed each in turn, and drank in the sweet smell of their warm skin, fighting the temptation to gather them in my arms and hug them 'til they cried for mercy. As I stroked Sean's curls, a golden halo against the white of his pillow, I thought of Aefe, my fiery-haired sister with the fiery temper to match. I saw her as she stood in the sea at Seapoint, her hair wet and plastered to her face, her eyes dull and lifeless as though a light had been switched off inside her head. I felt again the resistance in her arm as I tried to push her hand away to allow Fionuala to float to the surface. I saw Ma as she walked back along the beach, clutching Fionuala's shivering body, and I knew that what had happened that day had changed our family forever.

From the doorway I glanced back at Sean and Joseph, snug and safe in untroubled sleep. As I switched off the light a shiver of anxiety swept over me.

Mick, the big sap, was never here when I needed him.

*

Fionuala slipped a note into Joseph's birthday card. 'I've decided to write to Aefe and tell her we'll visit the next time I'm over. What do you think?'

It was August 1979 so I didn't have time to think. I was trying to adjust to the idea of Sean starting school. Buying his school uniform was a nightmare. Every purchase brought on a fit of crying. Sean was in danger of drowning in a sea of tears. Every time I looked at him my lip trembled and I grabbed him to my breast and sobbed. Eventually, he refused to come anywhere near me unless his father was in the room.

Anyway, I didn't want to go to Clare to see Aefe. I didn't want to talk to her about the past. I didn't want her to tell me what she was thinking, or what she was doing as my little sister fought for her life in the foamy water.

When I looked at my own brood as they bit and clawed each other, screamed with laughter or played in companionable silence the conviction grew that I didn't want to know what happened that day. Fionuala's obsession with the past would have to remain her obsession. I knew all I wanted to know: had all I wanted with Mick and the kids. So I ignored the note.

*

I was relieved that Fionuala didn't come home for Christmas. But then, on Little Christmas evening, as we were taking down the decorations and the kids were bursting balloons and strangling each other with lengths of tinsel, James phoned. 'She was rushed to hospital,' he said. 'It happened when I was on nights. She's always found nights difficult, but thank God I found her in time. I don't know what to do anymore. She's tried everything: counselling, medication, but nothing works. Living here doesn't help. It's been hard going for the Irish since the pub bombings.'

'But that was five years ago,' I said foolishly, recoiling from the image of Fionuala fighting for her life far from home.

'These things are not easily forgotten,' he said. 'Besides the doctors think it's personal. They say it might help if she talks to the family about what's troubling her.'

*

Another note arrived from Fionuala, the writing faint and spidery on the cream paper. 'I'm enclosing a letter I've written to Aefe. If you think it's all right could you please post it to her?'

I put the letter away, hid it in my undies drawer. A week later as I was threatening the kids with every torture known to man, Mick put the letter in my hand. 'Either answer it or throw it away,' he said, 'but don't take it out on the kids.'

Trembling with fright, I posted the letter.

*

Fionuala must have been listening when Da insisted that we can't hope to understand the present without recourse to the past. It seems she couldn't ignore the significance of the flight of the siblings — Aefe to

Clare, Aden to sea, herself to Birmingham and my own desperate dash into the arms of Mick O'Sullivan.

So we three sisters will meet and sift through the ashes of the past my mother tried so hard to bury. Aefe, Fionuala and me in one room, talking about Ma!

Trust Aden to be messing about in boats when I really need him.

PART II

Coming Home

We'd been sitting in our corner in The Green Man, having a few bevies as far away as we could get from the gaming machines, when dick-head Brian started talking about school. Why is it, when you've done football, women, politics, football, someone has to blabber on about what happened at school? 'Do you remember,' he asked, 'when we made Mrs. Dunne cry? What a tart she was. What a stupid tart.'

'No she wasn't,' said Kev. 'We were just a bunch of wankers: typical teenage wankers.'

'Uh, hark at Mister Sensitive,' Mark chipped in. 'Got in touch with your feminine side, have you Kev?'

'Piss off, pillock,' said Kev. 'It's time you grew up.'

It was all the way downhill from there. The stories about secondary school slid into reminiscences about primary school and then we really hit rock bottom — Mark said, 'Do you remember your first day at school?' By chucking out time, he was slobbering into the dregs of his pint. 'When my Mum left me, when she said good-bye that first morning, I sobbed my little heart out,' he sobbed. 'It was fuckin' awful.' Tears, beer and spittle settled into the cleft on his chin and he gave a thick, wet sniff, but there was no shutting him up. 'I felt so abandoned. It was the worst moment

Coming Home

of my life. I wanted my Mum. I didn't want anyone else. I just wanted my Mum,' he blubbed.

'Right lads, I'm off,' I said. While I'd still some functioning grey matter, I decided to make my escape and leave the others to do an Oprah on Mark.

I hesitated at the door and glanced back at the three blokes who'd been my mates since reception class. Kev's arm circled Mark's shoulders in a comforting hug. Brian took a deep swig from his beer, looked towards me, gave a knowing wink and then raised his glass in farewell. For a split second I thought, 'he knows.' But he couldn't know. I hadn't told anyone about the letter except Mum and Alistair.

I nodded my goodbye, pulled the door open, and left.

*

After the steamy warmth of the pub the raw night air hit me a slap on the face that nearly sent me reeling. I zipped up my jacket, pulled the collar close round my neck, hunched my shoulders against the cold and began the long trek home.

Christ! I was glad to be out of that. Mark's drunken ramblings were only bearable if you were bladdered yourself, and I needed to stay sober. Next day I was leaving, heading off, branching out. No more crappy job, no more seeing The Villa hammered. No more twice-weekly drinking sessions or playing Sunday League football with my best mates.

I was twenty-five. It was time to sort things out.

*

Unlike Mark, my memories of the first day of school are not tainted by sobbing and wailing. My misery started the next day, it lasted for years, and it had nothing to do with school.

When I can be bothered to scrape away all the shit of subsequent years and bring that day into focus, I remember an initial excitement and then a feeling of relief. There was apprehension and fear as well, but because my Dad told me that school would be my own special place where I could play with loads of kids and learn loads of new things, I was definitely excited.

I remember my Mum and I set off early that day. When we reached Chester Road I grabbed her hand. It was firm and comforting. We went through the kerb drill, looking left, right and left again and then crossed the busy road when all was clear.

I knew I looked smart. The neighbours we met said so. They said how my uniform suited me. The white shirt, grey jumper and trousers, the black blazer, all showed my blonde hair and fair complexion to advantage. My chest pumped up like a pigeon's at these compliments. I would break someone's heart some day they said. 'No I won't,' I said, but my Mum shushed me. I didn't want to break anyone's heart. The image of a broken, bleeding heart made me want to puke.

Grown-ups were weird. They didn't always make sense.

*

Coming Home

By the time we got to the junction of Hurst Lane there were hundreds of kids and their mothers heading in the same direction. The kids were making a hell of a racket. I tightened my grip on my Mum's hand. As we were caught up in the noisy crowd the excitement and anticipation started to leak away.

When we reached the school gates I was like a zombie. My eyes were wide and staring and I felt my stomach sloshing around inside, like when you've had too many bevies too quickly. People were coming at us from all directions and as my Mum led me into the school I felt them close in on me like a tall, dark forest.

Through the main doors the hall was high and wide like a church. The wooden floors were shiny and if you weren't careful you could slip and fall over, so I held my Mum's hand with all my skinny might. I liked the strong smell of polish — it reminded me of my Gran's wardrobe where she kept my presents. The walls were covered with the same crappy pictures I produced at home and that Mum liked to think were the first offerings of an artistic genius.

*

I'd visited the school twice before — once with my Mum and Dad and then again with my Mum. The first time my Mum and Dad turned into a pair of morons. They didn't speak until spoken to; they smiled at Mrs. Brown and nodded in agreement at her every word. My parents had regressed before my eyes and it was bloody scary.

At home I was used to being shushed or just plain ignored, but not in this magical place. Here I was actively encouraged to speak. Even when I stammered I was praised. 'An active mind,' beamed Mrs. Brown. 'His tongue can't keep up with the speed of his thoughts. He's a very bright boy.'

I expected my Dad to blow like a horse and snort, 'What a bleedin' load of crap,' and my Mum to shout, 'You watch your language.' Not on that day. They just sat smiling at each other as though they'd been glugging for hours.

*

Most of the time I try to avoid looking back. No point to it. Makes you feel either sad or angry. Check out Mark. Always ends up blubbering when he talks about the past. When I do indulge, when I allow myself to think about the early days before everything went pear-shaped, my most vivid memory is of feeling panicky when my Mum and Dad seemed to lose the plot.

With my Dad it happened when he'd had a few and he insisted on kissing and cuddling everyone in sight and when, usually on a Saturday night, he kept going up and down to the lav and kept stumbling on the stairs. When I got upset my Mum swore on a stack of bibles that he was just tired, but she was the world's worse liar, my Mum. Even as a five year old I knew she was having me on.

My Mum's little escapades were not as regular as my Dad's but they unnerved me just the same. Every

Coming Home

now and then she would find something so bleedin' funny she'd laugh so hard that she'd have to run to the lav in case she wet herself.

No kid should have to put with that kind of pressure.

*

I can tell you, I was glad to leave my Dad at home for the second visit to the school. There was some chance my Mum would behave like a reasonable human being without him.

On that day there was no one in the big entrance hall and I was spooked by the quiet and the emptiness that magnified every sound. I thought I could hear the ocean in my ear: a friggin' miracle, as we were over a hundred miles from the sea. My shoes made a terrible racket on the wooden floor. The echo bounced off the walls and I was certain we were being stalked by a giant. I was glad to get out of there and into the gym where we sat in a circle with other kids and mums. The chairs was small: I could sit right back and put my feet on the floor but my Mum was folded up like a frog ready to hop. All the other mothers were in the same predicament so I wasn't bothered.

Mr. Long (well-named as it happened — a long, skinny string of misery if ever there was one) organized games for everyone. Mums and kids pelted up and down the gym for a wheelbarrow race, an egg and spoon race (except we had potatoes), a relay race, and then musical chairs. Even then I hated all that competitive shit: it made me feel anxious and hyper. But my Mum and I won the wheelbarrow race and I nearly won the musical chairs expect a big, fat kid knocked me flying.

I knew my third visit to the school would be special. I'd be allowed to wear my new uniform. I was ecstatic. Adults don't half brainwash kids. They'd convinced me that the nerdy, grey kegs, the oversized blazer, the white shirt and the grotty tie were the hallmarks of maturity. It didn't take long before I hated that uniform.

When I moved to secondary school I had to wear the same cruddy clothes — only the tie and badge changed. Over the years I found a dozen ways to subvert it, culminating in the memorable day when Kev, Brian, Mark and myself turned up for school in shorts, Hawaiian shirts, straw hats and shades. The shit really hit the fan! It was bostin.

By then I was older and wiser.

*

On my first 'proper' day at school I knew I'd take a packed lunch and that my Mum would leave me after I'd completed the registration process. I also knew that she'd come and collect me at two o'clock, precisely.

There'd been some discussion as to who should accompany me on this auspicious occasion. At the time I didn't understood all that went on, but my Dad declared, 'Sometimes a boy needs his Dad, not a soppy, sentimental female who'll just upset him.'

My mother started to cry and wailed, 'He's not a boy: he's my baby and you're a pig.' I remember wanting to protest at this — my being a baby, that is — but sensibly I'd remained schtumm — it doesn't do to get between adults when they're emotional.

My Dad looked sad and said, 'I'm sorry. I'm sorry. Of course you're right. You take him.'

I was completely flummoxed by my Dad's reaction at the time. Usually when my Mum called my Dad a pig he went ballistic.

You have to admit, that miserable bastard Larkin had a point about parents.

*

I did my best to lighten the tense atmosphere in the house that morning by banging my drum and blowing my bugle, but it didn't work. I was told to stop being a baby and to act my age. I was a rising five, for Christ sake!

After breakfast my Dad decided to play his favourite game. He picked me up and threw me in the air. I hated when he did this. I was terrified that I'd hit my head off the ceiling; that he wouldn't catch me as I plunged towards the floor. Most of all I hated the way my stomach leapt into my head and left an empty space in my middle. I put up with it because my Dad seemed to really enjoy larking about, but I was always relieved when my Mum's refrain, 'It'll end it tears,' made him stop.

It should be compulsory for parents to grow up before they have kids.

Just before he jumped in the car and left for work that morning, my Dad knelt down beside me, straightened my tie and said, 'You're a big boy now, son, and you're moving on. From here on in you'll have a place of your own to go to every day — just like your Dad.' Then he folded me in his arms, held me tightly and kissed the top of my head — softly, gently, and the smell of his aftershave, strong and spicy, made me cough.

Over the years I've tried to recapture that smell. When I was ten and my Gran gave me money for my birthday I went to Boots and sniffed every bottle of aftershave on display, but before I could find the right one the security man ran me off. 'Dirty little pervert,' he shouted angrily as I scuttled away. I hadn't a clue what he meant at the time.

I still don't know what the creep was on about.

*

As Mum and I stood in the school hall, surrounded by more kids and adults than I'd ever seen before and I realized that I was going to be left in this huge place all on my own, my Dad's encouraging words didn't comfort me. I wanted to cry. My lower lip was out of control, jumping and jutting like a bleedin jack-in-the-box and I could feel the tears rushing to my eyes. I let go my Mum's hand and put my arms round her legs. I tried to bury my head in her dress but she was kitted out in a miniskirt so my head got stuck between her legs.

I knew my Mum was talking to me and that she was giggling but I couldn't really hear what she was saying so I continued to hang on. In an attempt to free herself she stepped backwards and her foot slipped on the shiny floor. She stumbled and fell with a resounding wallop and I went with her. On our way down we bumped into several people. Their books and bags flew all over the shop.

It was pandemonium! Kids rushed around trying to collect their gear. Most of them ended up with my Mum and me on the floor. The latecomers who came dashing through the front door added to the tangle of arms and legs and there we were — bang in the middle of the mess.

I clung like a barnacle to my Mum's legs. I was scared. I thought she'd really lose it because I'd made her look stupid. I knew she wouldn't shout at me in a public place, but her face would go stiff and her eyes empty and I hated that more than anything. I still hate when she does that. I was also scared that the teachers would go bananas because of the huge mess I'd made.

I didn't want to be in this place. I wanted my Dad. I wanted him to hold me in his strong arms as he'd done earlier that day.

*

The limbs I was clinging to were shaking and trembling. I thought my Mum was hurt, that she was crying. I expected to see tears streaming down her cheeks but when I untangled myself and stood up I could see that her lips were clamped tightly together and her face was scrunched up as she fought for control. Then her jaws slackened, her mouth opened and she made a gurgling sound. Half-sitting, half-lying, her head snapped back and a loud, raucous laugh filled the large space.

I was definitely relieved that she was all right, but bloody hell, man, I was also definitely terrified. I knew that my Mum was about to give vent to one of her laughing fits.

No one really understood the reasons for her uncontrolled bouts of mirth. I'd heard my Dad say, 'It seems to me, sweetheart, that your imagination suffers fits of spontaneous combustion,' but that didn't mean shit to me then and I still don't really understand it now.

I hated when my Mum had one of her hysterical flings. She was so taken with the joke that she forgot I was there. It made me feel lonely. And there was always the chance that she might wet herself — right there, in the school, where everyone could see.

All the kids clambered to their feet, dusted themselves off, collected their belongings and rushed to assembly. I grabbed hold of my Mum's hand and pulled with all my might. 'Get up, Mum. Get up,' I pleaded. I managed to move her to a sitting position, but because she was stuffed with laughter she flapped about like a boneless chicken. I was begging her to make an effort when Mr. Long arrived on the scene. By this time I was dying with embarrassment. I prayed my Mum would vanish in a puff of smoke.

I was flooded with relief as Mr. Long did the trick. He helped her to her feet and saw her off the premises, then he took my hand and led me to my new classroom.

*

There were about fifteen kids already in the classroom, most of them hushed and staring at the great pillock who was wailing and shouting for his mum. That was my first sighting of Mark. Twenty years on and he's still a big, slobbering git.

I sat next to him when we opened our lunch boxes and started to eat our sarnies, except Mark didn't have any sarnies. I can still feel my eyes stretching wider and wider as he stuffed his red, puffy face with two packets of crisps — one ready salted and one cheese and onion — a Mars bar, a Penguin and a can of Pepsi. I knew I wanted to be his friend. 'Why were you crying?' I asked. He opened his mouth and his lower lip jutted out and started to quiver.

I'd made a tactical mistake so I hurried on. 'This is our special place,' I said, 'so there's no need to cry. My Dad said we're moving on.' That stopped him in mid-sniffle. His mouth stayed open but his lip stopped trembling. Playing the advantage I asked, 'Can I be your friend?' He couldn't answer — his gob was too full — but as melting chocolate dribbled onto his chin he nodded his head and the deal was done.

*

I opened the door of my flat and nearly tripped over the suitcase and rucksack, packed ready for my early start the next day. The image of Mark crying and slobbering into his beer came back to me. He'd phone tomorrow, wanting to know if we were going to the usual place for a few bevies after work, but I wouldn't be here.

I should have told him and Kev and Brian about my plans. I knew I should. They'd been my best mates for as long as I could remember and, in a way, it was because of them that I had the bottle to do what I planned. Without the certainty of their friendship, the knowledge that they'd always be there, I knew I wouldn't be able to take the risk I was about to take.

They'd be pissed off when they found out I'd gone, but they'd know that I had a good reason for not letting them in on my plans. That's how it is with blokes, you don't have to share your every thought, talk about your feelings: they give you space, don't judge you.

I'd wanted to tell them, but I was afraid they'd talk me out of it: that I'd agree to stay. Worse still, they might want to come with me. I didn't want that. I knew this was something I had to do on my own.

*

Mum collected me as she'd promised at the end of my first day at school. I waited excitedly for Dad to come home, running to the window every time I heard a car. I couldn't wait to tell him about Mum and me slipping on the floor: to hear him laugh at the chaos we'd caused. I wanted to tell him that he was right: that school was my special place; that we had swings and a slide and a sandpit INDOORS. Most of all I wanted

Coming Home

to tell him about my new friend Mark and his scrumptious food.

At eight o'clock Mum put me to bed, promising to wake me when Dad arrived.

But he never came home again. It seems he'd found his own special place with a special someone in tow.

*

When my Dad was with us I'd hated my Mum's fits of spontaneous mirth, but when they stopped after he disappeared I missed them, would have given anything to have them back: to see her helpless with laughter instead of tears.

I was glad when Alistair arrived on the scene and they got married. I was pleased when my little sister and brother were born. It was good to hear Mum laugh again, even if it meant she was in danger of wetting herself.

*

The letter arrived a year ago, almost nineteen years to the day when I first started school. I put it in my stamp album: placed it, unopened, between the pages where Dad and I had stuck my Australian stamps.

Every day for about a month I opened the album and stared at the sealed envelope and then put it away again.

'Read it,' Mum said. 'You should read it, sweetheart.' And I did.

So I'm going to find my Dad: to see the special place that had lured him away from us.

Mum doesn't mind. Thanks to Alistair she moved on a long time ago. Now it's my turn.

*

It was dark and cold and the crescent moon was still glowing white as I pulled the door shut early the next morning. I picked up my suitcase, threw my rucksack over my shoulder and walked down the path towards the waiting taxi.

I smiled to myself, pleased with the notion that if things didn't work out down-under Mark, Kev and Brian would still be here, in good old Brum, when I came back. If things went all right they could come and visit and we could go bungee-jumping off Sydney Bridge with my Dad.

The thought of Mark, trusses stretched across his fat belly as he prepared to plunge hundreds of feet towards the water of Sydney Harbour, screaming for his Mum, made me laugh out loud.

'Someone's pleased to be leaving,' the voice of the taxi-driver emerged from the dark of his cab, grumpy from lack of sleep.

'Why not?' I said. 'There's no reason to be unhappy about going away, mate. It doesn't have to be for good, you know. Leaving can be the prelude to coming home.'

I loaded my luggage into the back of the car and climbed into the seat next the driver.

'Have it your way, mate,' he said.

Coming Home

'That's the plan,' I said', 'that's the plan.'

Guardian Angel

She was tired. It had been a long, exhausting day, and it wasn't over yet. The strangeness of the countryside, blurred and flattened by the speed of the coach, made her feel nervous and unsure. She longed for the home she'd left that morning: she longed for Luka. Already she was missing the children.

*

The coach, which was now hurtling along the M1 towards Birmingham, had been held up in the choking traffic of London and was running late. She was scared. What if she arrived too late? Where would she spend the night? She had two telephone numbers, one in Birmingham and her back-up number in Bristol, but her Birmingham contact would be difficult to reach unless she phoned before six. She didn't have a mobile and by the time she'd found the public phones in Victoria she'd run out of time and had made a mad dash to catch the coach.

She wasn't sure she had enough money for a night's lodgings. The price of the bottle of water and sandwich she'd bought at the airport made her gasp in amazement. Her confidence in her ability to make herself understood had been severely undermined by her attempts at the airport and coach station. Her

English, which at home she used with ease and not a little pride, seemed rudimentary and awkward.

A slim man with short, blonde hair had talked to her at Victoria Station and she couldn't make sense of what he'd said. As she stood attempting to get her bearings, he walked briskly towards her, smiled a dazzling smile and said, 'A room for the night, duck? She knew two definitions of duck: the noun, which named a water fowl and the verb, which described a quick movement of the head or body to avoid a blow. Neither made sense in this context, but, instinctively, she ducked her head and saw that the man had bent to pick up her suitcase which was wedged between her legs. She clenched her knees and locked the case more firmly. He grabbed the handle and pulled, but she held on. 'Stupid bitch,' he said, his smile vanishing. But he gave up the struggle, turned away and pushed through the crowded waiting area.

'It don't do to talk to strangers, love,' a women who'd witnessed the encounter said, her pale, wrinkled face puckered with concern. 'You sit next to me and you'll be all right.'

Natasha smiled wanly, sat down, took a notebook and pencil from her bag and under the printed heading 'NEW WORDS' she wrote the word 'duck' As an afterthought, although she was unsure of the spelling, she added the word 'bitch'. Then she left her case in the care of the woman and went on her futile search for a phone.

*

She looked at her watch. It read twenty to five, and she didn't know how far they were from Birmingham. In fact she didn't know the right time. She'd adjusted her watch as instructed on the plane, but every clock she'd seen since showed a different time. She'd almost stopped breathing on catching sight of the clock when she boarded the coach: it read four thirty and they hadn't yet left London.

In her panic she couldn't remember the words to ask for the time. Sweating, she searched in her bag for her dictionary; silently practised the phrase and had plucked up courage to speak to the women next to her when she once again glanced at the clock. It had obviously stopped: it still read four thirty.

*

As they neared Birmingham the traffic grew heavier. The coach was hemmed in on all sides. Every lane of the M6 was packed with cars, trucks and other coaches. She looked at her watch again. Five forty-five. She'd never make it to the city centre by six o'clock. Even if she did she'd still have to find a phone and figure out how to use it.

The sun shone hotly through the coach window. There was no curtain so she couldn't avoid its blinding light and blistering heat. She dabbed at the perspiration on her forehead and upper lip. She felt moisture creeping down her back and from her armpits. As sweat poured from her she felt her mouth crack with dryness. She unscrewed the bottle-top and dribbled some lukewarm water onto her tongue. She

Guardian Angel

moistened her dry lips and wondered when she'd next have a shower.

Despite the anxiety that clenched her stomach and stiffened her back, her attention was caught by the hustling scene unfolding around her. Motor vehicles of every shape, size and colour tangoed through the hot city streets. Bumper to bumper they moved forward slowly, halted briefly and then hurled themselves towards an empty stretch of road. The grinding and screeching of brakes filled the air as the vehicles came to a juddering halt: then they were off again, tyres squealing and burning as the workers of Birmingham tried to escape the steaming city.

To her left, panes of glass, framed by the hot, red doors of the West Midlands Fire Station, blinked tiredly in the early-evening sunshine. Blocks of flats stretched skywards as though longing to escape the fumes and noise. All round her the roads were an intricate tangle of flyovers and underpasses. To her right, as though hurled into place by a vindictive giant, a random scattering of modern buildings fragmented the summer skyline.

*

The coach driver bullied his way into the right-hand lane, and with a flourish, swung the vehicle into Rea Street and then into the grim interior of Digbeth Coach Station.

It was half-past six. Natasha stood, hot and bemused in the bleak, concrete arena. She didn't know what to do. 'When you are in a strange place you must look as though you are confident. You must look as though you know what to do.' Luka's words echoed in her head. Before she left home that morning nine-year-old Eva had hugged her tightly and whispered, 'Your guardian angel will take care of you, Mama.' Natasha hadn't told her daughter that she didn't believe in guardian angels.

She picked up her case and walked towards the waiting room. People stood in groups talking and laughing or lounged on the tough, plastic seating.

Natasha scanned the room several times before she spotted the public telephones. She walked towards them, read the instructions carefully — twice — and with coins at the ready she dialled the Birmingham number. There was no ringing sound, just the continuous purring of the dialling tone. Her mouth filled with salty saliva. She felt slightly dizzy. She hadn't considered this possibility. The phone couldn't be out of order — this was England! She went through the procedure again, with the same result. The sweat gathered on her upper lip. She replaced the receiver and re-read the instructions. She almost laughed aloud with relief. She needed to insert the coins before dialling.

This time the phone rang, but the forlorn ringing continued unanswered. They weren't there. They'd gone. She'd known the chances of making contact after six were slim, but she was bitterly disappointed. Sweat oozed from under her arms and down her spine. Her body seemed to be dissolving slowly, liquefying in the oppressive heat of the airless room.

She shook her head to dispel the dizziness. She had to look confident. Luka had told her, 'You must look assured.'

She located the women's toilets. The space was drab and functional with grey walls, chipped earthenware and cracked floor tiles. A wire bin spewed the overflow of used paper towels onto the floor. She pulled a towel from the dispenser and cleaned the washbasin. She filled the basin, removed her blouse and splashed her face, neck and arms with cold, refreshing water, patting herself dry with a fresh towel. She took her toothbrush and toothpaste from her handbag and brushed her teeth. She replaced her blouse, combed her damp hair and applied lipstick to her parched lips. Studying her face in the mirror, she took a deep breath, picked up her case and returned to the waiting room.

*

She sensed she was being watched. She glanced around the room as casually as she could. A man with a large, white turban sitting proudly on his tiny head, his grey beard covering his chest like a hairy napkin, was staring at her with unabashed curiosity. 'All Britain's problems are caused by the ethnic diversity of its population,' Luka had declaimed. 'You must avoid these people.' She wasn't sure which people he meant, and she hadn't bothered to ask. She'd felt, instinctively, that the answer would confuse her. At home it was simple — you avoided the gypsies. But with such a mixed population, how could she decide who to trust and who to avoid? Luka would know, but he wasn't here.

Natasha turned her back on the man and busied herself dialling the Bristol number. The phone rang once, twice, three times. 'Please answer the phone, please, please answer,' she prayed.

'Hello!' The voice was young and male.

She spoke slowly and clearly. 'May I speak to Olga, please?'

'Hangonasec,' the young man said, and Natasha froze with horror. He didn't speak English; and she hadn't recognised the language.

'Olgaphoneforyou! Olgaph..o..o..one!' the young man bellowed.

'Hello, Olga speaking.'

'Olga, it's Natasha.'

'Natasha! Where are you?'

'I'm in Birmingham.'

'You've made it! You've made it!'

'Olga, I'm scared. I don't know what to do.'

Natasha listened carefully to Olga's instructions. She replaced the receiver, picked up her case, walked to the seat nearest the telephone and sat down.

Once again she wet her cracked lips with the tepid water. She answered the grumblings of her empty stomach by eating the dried remains of her sandwich.

To her right she felt a stirring of the damp, paralysing air. She looked blankly in that direction, her mind still preoccupied with Olga's words. The man with the white turban was standing next to her, a toothless smile on his hairy face. 'Are yow all roight, bab?' he asked.

'I am o.k. thank you,' Natasha spoke slowly and carefully, without looking at the man.

'Oi couldn't help noticing that yow seem to be having trouble with the phone, loike.'

'I am o.k. thank you,' Natasha repeated.

'Oi'd be ploised to help if Oi can,' he persisted.

'I am waiting for a call, thank you.'

'All roight bab,' said the little man, but if yow need any help Oi'm just over there. Don't yow be afraid to ask, all roight?'

As the man returned to his seat Natasha closed her eyes, took a deep breath and slowly released it. She mustn't panic. He seemed kind, but he belonged to an ethnic minority and Luka had warned her to be careful. Besides, she'd rather talk to a native speaker.

Ten minutes later Natasha was still waiting patiently for the phone to ring when the man returned.

'Oi've just thought, bab,' he said, 'them phones don't toike incoming calls.'

It took a few minutes and the intervention of another traveller, but eventually Natasha understood that if she wanted to speak to Olga again she'd have to make the call.

'Natasha, thank god! I've been trying to get through. I've got the information for you. Write this down. A-v-o-n-c-r-o-f-t H-o-u-s-e on the H-a-g-l-e-y R-o-a-d. Got that?'

'Yes.'

'Don't worry about paying I've sorted that out. Have you enough money for a taxi?'

'I think so.'

'All right. Phone me when you get there.'

'Yes, yes, I will. Thank you Olga. Thank you.'

'Good luck,' Olga said and then the line went dead.

*

Natasha felt sweat sidle down her inner arms. She could feel her feet moist and damp inside her shoes. Sweat drenched her forehead and upper lip. She searched her pockets for a tissue and dabbed at herself until it congealed into small, sodden lumps. She opened her hand and looked at the wet tissue. She made a fist round it and squeezed hard. The movement released the tears that flowed in abundance down her face.

She lowered her head and stumbled towards her case. She slumped onto the seat, keeping her head bowed. A great sob sloshed though her. She sniffed loudly, and with the backs of her hands wiped away the tears. The longing for home was pure physical pain. She wanted Luka: she wanted her children.

'Yow all roight bab?' The familiar voice was comforting.

Natasha looked up at the cheery face. 'I am all right soon,' she said. I want a taxi.'

'Where are yow gowing?'

'Near to here,' Natasha said.' I am all right.'

'Oi'll help yow, bab. Yow don't look too hot to me.'

Guardian Angel

She assured the little man that she was very hot indeed. In fact she was finding the mid-summer heat of Birmingham overpowering.

When they emerged from the station into the dusty heat of Digbeth there wasn't a taxi to be seen. Mr. Singh looked at the address Natasha had written down, assured her that it was no distance and that he would have to pass it on his way home to Smethwick. He would drop her off. Natasha's brain tried to sort out how, and from what, Mr.Singh would drop her. She gave up the struggle, and followed him, once again, through the grimy, bleakness of the bus station, out the other side to where his car was parked.

*

For the second time that day Natasha was driven through the tangle of hot Birmingham Streets. Mr.Singh was a confident driver and he dealt with the constant flow of fast-moving traffic with verve and panache. 'Oi'll take yow up Broad Street, bab, and yow can have a look at the new Brum.'

Mr. Singh's use of English was, for the most part, beyond her comprehension. It was not the English used at The British Council in Kosice where she had started her language lessons, but then he wasn't a native of the country so it was little wonder he spoke such peculiar English. She understood very little of what he said, but she'd found it didn't matter.

She couldn't wait to get to her destination. She could almost feel the gushing water of the hot shower bouncing off her tired body. She would ring Olga. She would not rush to ring Luka: it was way past the children's bedtime so she wouldn't get to speak to them that night and she needed time to consider what to tell Luka of her day. She would shower, have something to eat and then ring him.

She didn't think she'd tell him about Mr. Singh just yet. He'd become agitated and angry that she'd ignored his advice about ethnic minorities. But Luka hadn't been to England so there were some things he didn't understand.

*

Natasha drifted into an exhausted sleep and dreamt of a small, hairy angel with a white, turban-like halo encircling his head in a glowing light. He floated gently round and round the waiting room in Digbeth Coach Station, skimming the heads of the people who stood or sat in the dingy surroundings, a gummy smile lighting up his face. Children waved to him; adults grinned. No one seemed perturbed by his actions. No one seemed to wonder why he was there.

Significant Moments

It was warm for April: a sprightly, warm, spring afternoon and Orla pottered around her garden, enjoying the caress of the sun on her back. Next door the children shouted and squealed, running aimlessly up and down the overgrown lawn. A couple of seconds silence allowed her to hear the faint ringing of the phone. She ran, dropping her garden gloves on the way.

'Hello,' she gasped.

'Are you o.k.?' Charles sounded slightly mocking.

'Yes, fine. I've just run a three-minute mile so I'm a little breathless.'

'You must be getting old.' She could hear the grin in his voice. 'Just to let you know that there's some celebration or other over here and the High Street's closed to traffic, so you'll need to avoid it. '

'How do I do that?'

'I don't know; come round the back way; you could check the A-Z. You figure it out, woman, I'm coping with the cooking,' he laughed.

*

She lowered herself into the bath with a grateful sigh. She hadn't done much gardening, but still her limbs craved warmth and comfort. Charles was right — she was getting old. Trust a man to state the obvious. Every bugger on the planet ages from the moment of birth, but he had to point to her advancing years. Tactless sod! But it had jangled a nerve. She had a strong feeling that age was a significant issue for Charles and if it was she was sunk.

It was time to go. The early evening was still warm and sunny and she felt quite festive as she left the house, clutching wine from her recent visit to Italy.

She prolonged her glance in the rear-view mirror in order to check her hair and face. Her grey hair was lightly streaked with black and her blue eyes were framed by a halo of fine lines. 'Yeah, but I'm great fun,' she jeered at her reflection.

*

As she inched her way along Broad Street she smiled at the hundreds of skimpily-clad youngsters enjoying the spring evening. They jostled each other for standing room outside the cafes and bars which lined the pavement, they laughed and shouted and wandered nonchalantly from one side of the street to the other — oblivious of the ribbon of traffic which wound its way towards Five Ways.

'You can't be serious!' Charles had done nothing to hide his astonishment when she divulged her route.

'I know my way along the Hagley Road,' she'd said firmly, 'so that's the way I'm going.'

'But it's a cross-country trek, woman,' he'd insisted. 'Come along Dudley Road.'

Significant Moments

'I'm not familiar with Dudley Road,' she said, which was not, strictly speaking, true. When she'd first arrived in Birmingham she'd known Dudley Road rather well. Thirty years previously she'd made regular trips to the hospital. She clambered aboard the number eleven at Six Ways and an hour later crawled off the bus, green and puking and made her way to the antenatal clinic. With the advancement of her pregnancy and the enlargement of her belly the journey became more and more arduous, but she refused to cancel her appointments. Her visits to the bustling hospital were warm moments in a life cold with loneliness and isolation.

She decided to stick with the Hagley Road. Experience had taught her that circuitous routes one knew well were invariably less time-consuming than unfamiliar shortcuts. She was nervous about this evening so she didn't want to be late. Or perhaps she did want to be late? Perhaps she didn't want to get there at all?

One thing was sure, advancing years hadn't made her more decisive.

*

She'd met Charles six months previously, but hadn't really got a handle on him as yet. He was an intelligent man; fun to be with and she felt an undercurrent of warmth and attraction when she was with him. But physically the relationship was proving a no-no. She couldn't figure out if this was (a) because he was overly shy and needed more encouragement than she was willing to offer (b) because he was incapable of physical intimacy (c) because he was gay (she thought this unlikely; she'd never fancied a gay fella) (d) because she was so old and decrepit that no-one would find her attractive ever again or (e) if he was what her dear daughter called a 'commitment-phoebe' — a supposedly new breed of man who refused to abandon his mates and the single life in favour of settling down with a woman.

Whatever the cause, Orla had decided during her time in Italy that today would be a significant milestone in their relationship. She hoped that several weeks' separation would add the spark that would finally ignite the flame of passion. She'd decided that she couldn't afford to hang around any longer to see if he would thaw under the heat of her radiant charms.

Being perfectly honest, her radiance was dimming at an alarming rate so she didn't have time to mess about.

*

Too late, she remembered how much she hated the Hagley Road. Most of the drivers seemed to think they were stuntmen, escapees from the latest, most daring, action film. As cars whizzed by, her heart started to pound. A burning sensation crept from the base of her neck to her face and to the top of her head. Her cheeks flushed red-hot and she thought her skull would pop. Just what she needed — to arrive at Mr. Cool's looking like a turkey on heat.

Significant Moments

Despite the urgent need to concentrate her peripheral vision registered familiar landmarks and memories flooded back, blocking the rising tide of road-panic. Her mouth pulled into a wide grin as she slowed down at a red light. She was sixteen years younger, it was midnight and she was driving along Monument Road. In a moment of madness she and a friend convinced themselves that they could recapture their youth by going to the Tower Ballroom.

'God that was depressing, I don't know why I ever listen to you,' Una had exclaimed, as they drove home in Orla's battered Mini. Orla's jaw dropped and she glanced at her friend in amazement, taking her eyes off the road for a split second.

'It was your idea,' she spluttered.

When Orla looked again, she discovered she was travelling too fast to make the sharp left needed to avoid the one-way street ahead. She was hurtling towards a small island with a very deep kerb that had been placed in the middle of the road to block the way forward and which she was about to mount at break-neck speed.

'Hold on, she'd shouted as the car surged onto the island. The front wheels hit the concrete with a resounding smack and the car lurched to one side. For an interminable moment it rocked alarmingly, but it stayed upright and continued its trajectory. Orla's head bounced off the ceiling and she heard the scraping of the exhaust pipe as the car thumped and thudded onto the road. Una's screams filled the tiny space.

GILDED SHADOWS

Back on level ground, Orla was aware of a group of people on the pavement to her left. They had just left the Lychee Restaurant and were strung out like Chinese lanterns along the pavement, their faces luminescent in the dark. They stood transfixed, eyes staring in disbelief, mouths wide open.

And her problems were not yet over. She was going the wrong way up a one-way street. She needed to join the Hagley Road and the set of traffic lights she was approaching didn't cater for her.

'Don't laugh,' she screamed, rather unnecessarily, at the petrified Una. 'Don't you dare laugh until we're safely out of this mess.'

In the end they'd both laughed — loud, raucous, belly-aching laughter. They had laughed until the tears ran in torrents down their cheeks, until they'd laughed themselves out. But they never went dancing again.

*

As the Strathallen Hotel loomed, circular and honeycombed on her right, a memory of a rather frightening moment with a man, young enough to be her son, shouted for attention, but she pushed it away. She needed to concentrate.

She had to position herself to take a right at Bearwood Road. It was still a fair distance away but at the speed she was forced to drive she'd end up in the Clents if she wasn't careful. She checked her mirror but realized she'd need the daring of a kamikaze to make the manoeuvre. Calm down, be patient, she told herself. An opportunity will present itself: be ready when it does.

She could feel the vice-like grip of tension as it spread from her shoulders to her neck and head. This was ridiculous. What had promised to be a pleasant, relaxing, perhaps, 'significant' evening might never happen because she couldn't get off the friggin' Hagley Road.

She reached Barnsley Road and checked her mirror once again. There was a break in the traffic but her rather desperate glance had clocked a four-wheel drive thundering towards the gap. Without thinking she indicated and manoeuvred simultaneously. Her recklessness was answered by the screeching of tyres and the blaring of horns and for one awful moment she almost closed her eyes. But she'd made it: she was in the right-hand lane, turning right into Bearwood Road.

From now on it would be a piece of cake.

*

She drove along at a leisurely pace and the tension seeped slowly away. Her thoughts drifted to the evening ahead and she felt a shiver of anticipation. Although she was nervous she was looking forward to seeing Charles. During her absence abroad she'd realized that she missed their times together.

She wasn't quite sure where the High Street began or ended or how to avoid it, so she pulled into the side of the road to check the A-Z. She rummaged in her bag but couldn't find her reading glasses. She peered at the page. Orange, yellow and white roads blurred into a hazy tangle. 'Sod it!' she exclaimed, throwing the book from her in disgust. She indicated and drove off once again.

The road forked right and left. To the left she could see shops and several dozen people milling about on the pavement and on the road. She hesitated, but couldn't see the barriers Charles had mentioned. Ahead of her cars inched forward so she assumed that the celebrations had all but ended and that she could reach her destination via the High Street.

The debris of the festivities was strewn liberally around: gutters were clogged with mounds of rubbish, discarded bottles and cans made intricate patterns on the road and pavement. Groups of young people, determined to continue the party, were laughing and dancing and larking about.

There were just two cars ahead of her and they continued to move forward slowly. Young men, assured and arrogant, kings of their turf, approached each car in turn and the vehicle stopped. The driver wound down the window, pleasantries were exchanged and the cars moved on.

It was Orla's turn. She felt a slight tingle of apprehension but she shooed it away. The five young men converging on her car were smiling and laughing; all round people stood watching, enjoying their high spirits.

The young men were singing and dancing and Orla smiled, brought the car to a halt, took her hands off the steering wheel and clapped in acknowledgement of their uninhibited enjoyment.

Two of the group jumped onto the bonnet. Two more put their hands on either side of the windscreen and started to rock the car. The fifth continued to gyrate, clap his hands and sing.

Orla's facial muscles tightened and her smile faded. As the rocking of the car became more and more violent she could feel fear and anger rise in equal measure. She opened the window a couple of inches. 'That's not funny,' she shouted. 'Stop it! It's frightening. It's not funny. Stop it!'

Beyond the five leering faces outside her windscreen, she was aware of many other faces. To her right a small crowd of young women and men stood, laughing, smiling and shouting encouragement. To her left people walked along the pavement looking straight ahead.

*

Orla's obvious alarm seemed to excite the young men. With renewed vigour they bounced on the bonnet and rocked the car. The dancer leaned his face close to the windscreen, smirked at Orla, grabbed the windscreen wiper and snapped it from its anchor. Laughing, he whirled and jumped, holding the wiper triumphantly aloft, before flinging it onto the road.

Orla started the engine. She depressed the clutch and found first gear. She put her foot gently on the accelerator and moved off slowly. Her tormentors jumped away from the car and she was free to go.

She had travelled about twenty feet when anger overcame fear. She stopped the car, got out and walked back along the road to look for the windscreen wiper. The five youths came towards her, continuing their wild, exuberant dance.

Too late she realized she'd made a dreadful mistake. Although her every instinct demanded flight, she forced herself to walk the short distance to her car as they swirled round her, jeering and taunting. The young man who'd snapped the wiper stood by the car door. When she tried to side-step him he put out his hand to touch her.

As his hand brushed her shoulder she was aware that some young people who'd encouraged his earlier exploits were no longer laughing. Their smiles froze: they looked uncertain, embarrassed. When she moved to avoid her molester she saw that several women on the pavement observed the scene, expressions dark with disapproval. But nobody spoke. Nobody intervened. The jeers and taunts of the young men were harsh and cruel against the silence, and her protests rang out frightened and lonely in the warm, evening air.

She felt his hand travel from her shoulder to her arm. As she swivelled to avoid him they were on her head and her back. 'Stop that!' she shouted, again and again. The fury in her voice surprised him and as he hesitated she somehow managed to sneak past him and into the car.

Significant Moments

She locked the door, started the engine and drove off. She kept her eyes on the road ahead. She didn't want to see what was to the right or left of her. At that moment, more than at any other in her relatively long life, she wanted to be folded lovingly in someone's arms: to stay there until the trembling stopped: to feel safe.

*

'You made it then?' Charles stood in the doorway, smiling. She followed him down the hallway and into the kitchen and offered him the wine. She tried to smile and return his banter, but her face was rigid with fright.

'Could I possibly have a drink?' she said, 'I've had a bit of a shock.'

Charles poured a generous measure of whiskey. Her voice was calm and flat as she told him what had happened. A flicker of concern flashed in his eyes and he took an involuntary step towards her. She waited for the comfort of his embrace. In mid-stride his eyes shut down, he checked his movement and the moment had gone.

*

Charles tried to persuade her to stay: to at least have something to eat before venturing out again, but she refused. 'I think it's best if I go now,' she said. 'They've forecast rain and I've only one wiper, so I best go now.'

He stood at the door and watched her as she climbed slowly into the car. He waved farewell as she drove off, but she didn't see him. She didn't look back. She kept her eyes focused on the road ahead.

A Fresh Start

My hand slid across the cold, slimy surface as I tried to find my rucksack in the pitch dark. I touched something soft and wet and squirmed in horror. A slug had made its way into my den! 'Where there's one slug there'll be hundreds, maybe thousands,' my Nan had told me. I imagined great piles of the oozing, black lumps in my rucksack, clinging to all my things, and I started to heave.

But I had to pull myself together. Everything I owned was in that rucksack and if I wanted them to think I'd really disappeared, had gone forever, so that they'd give up looking for me, I knew I had to leave it behind.

But I couldn't make up my mind. My head was too full: my thoughts all over the place. I couldn't think straight. I'd have to decide later — perhaps when I'd had a rest. I'd just lie down and rest, and then I'd make up my mind.

I zipped myself into my sleeping bag and lay there, invisible in the dense blackness, holding my head in both hands. Every now and then I heard footsteps above me, some slow and laborious, some light and quick. They were very close. If I put my hand through the concrete ceiling I could catch an ankle as it passed overhead. That'd surprise them: a hand rising from the stairs and grabbing them tightly, holding them still.

Things had come to an end here. I'd have to go somewhere else. I wanted to cry but I couldn't. It would take a flood of tears to get past the dry hard knot in my middle, but I didn't have any tears. I was dry inside: like flaky skin.

*

Not so long ago I'd felt good. It'd been wicked that day last summer when I'd made a fresh start: when things were going right.

I remember it was hot, really hot. My head was thumping from the heat. I stopped under the shade of the trees in front of the college and took a swig of water. I'd come to enrol on a course and I was nervous. The heat and the nerves made me dribble with sweat. I could feel the perspiration sliding between my shoulder blades and under my arms and the sensation made me shudder. I hate sweat: particularly on men. I hate sweaty men.

I'd come to enrol on a course. Not any old crap. Not that vocational stuff. No way. I'd read the prospectus and I wanted to enrol for A level English Language and Literature and A level History. They could keep the other rubbish. 'Always aim for the top,' my Dad said. 'Don't settle for second best, Princess.' And that's what I was going to do. I had a problem though and the thought of it made me sweat even more.

A Fresh Start

I followed the black arrows to Advice and Admission, to Screening, to the Form Completion Centre, to the Subject Specialist.

The hall was cold and gloomy. Even though it was hot outside the place smelt of damp, with an underlying stink of stale sweat. There weren't many people about, just a few stragglers here and there. 'Although this is the main enrolment period, we manage a system of continuous, open-access enrolment so you shouldn't have to wait very long,' the snooty cow on the phone had told me. 'Drop in at any time to suit yourself: we always try to accommodate clients,' she'd said, all posh and cheerful. Stuck up cow. I hate stuck up cows.

When my turn came I took my seat in front of the Subject Specialist. She was very thin with a long, pale face and lots of shaggy, ginger hair. I handed her my form. She glanced at it and then looked at me over her reading glasses.

'You've forgotten to complete this section,' she said, turning the form round so I could read it, and pointing with her pen to the empty space where my 'qualifications to date' should have been listed.

'Haven'tgotany,' I mumbled.

'I'm sorry, I didn't quite catch that.' She smiled encouragingly.

'I haven't got any,' I said.

'You have no qualifications?'

'No.'

She picked up the form and read it slowly and carefully. 'You're seventeen and you have no GCSEs,' she said. I didn't answer.

'You are applying to do A levels but you haven't got the necessary qualifications,' she said. 'You're too young to do that. At your age you need the appropriate qualifications before we allow progression to the next level. You'll have to enrol for GCSEs.'

I started to cry. My lower lip trembled and I sniffed and then sniffed again, really loudly. 'Use your handkerchief,' she said. I wiped my eyes and nose with the back of my hand. She shuddered slightly and handed me a tissue.

'What is it?' she asked. 'Why didn't you take GCSEs?'

'I couldn't,' I said. 'It was my Mum … my Dad … I couldn't.' I gave a great, sloppy sob.

'What grades did your teachers expect you to get?'

I cried harder. 'English was my best subject,' I said. 'I was the best in the class.'

'Well you shouldn't have any problems passing your GCSE and then you can enrol for A level next year.'

My head started to thump really loudly. My chest felt tight. I could hardly breathe. My face was cold and I could feel it turn pale.

'I have to do A levels.' I sobbed. 'My Dad says I can do A levels.'

She gave in eventually and enrolled me on a two-year course to do two GCSEs and two A levels.

A Fresh Start

I had to wait until the following Saturday to tell my Dad. I couldn't phone him until the weekend. He was never sure when he'd get home from work during the week and he didn't believe in mobile phones. 'They're an assault on our basic right to privacy,' he said. But I knew he'd be really, really pleased. 'You can do it, Princess.' That's what he always said to me. It didn't matter what I wanted to do, he always said, 'You can to it Princess.'

My Mum didn't agree. 'You need to be realistic,' she said. 'Forget your fancy ideas. You need to put food on the table first.'

When I left the college the sun was hotter than ever. I didn't want to go back to my place. I was too excited, too pleased with myself. I wanted to share it with someone, but I couldn't just pop in to see my Mum in case sweaty-balls was there, so I stood under the shade of the trees and took a swig of water, trying to decide what to do.

The cars on the Bristol Road raced past, their colours blurred as the hot sun bounced off hot metal. I waited for a gap and walked to the other side. The trees on Bourneville Lane were like huge, lacy umbrellas that left fancy patterns on the pavement. I walked underneath and the patterns danced on my feet, my arms and on my hands.

When I got to the pond I found a seat in the shade and stared at the thick, green water. Ducks swam slowly up and down. Geese waddled around the edge, adding another layer of droppings to the filthy concrete. The water and shit smelt gross. It was disgusting. At the far end of the pond two young mothers gave three young kids bread to throw to the birds. I hate people who do that. I hate soggy bread.

*

Induction the following week was crap. The college was heaving. There were people everywhere — all ages, all sizes, all colours.

I can't remember the details of that day. I know I was given a timetable and book lists; that I met lecturers and students; that I was taken on a tour of the building, but after the first ten minutes everything sort of merged together and didn't make much sense.

I waited 'til I got back to my place before reading the book lists. I nearly passed out when I saw the names of the authors. Chaucer, Shakespeare, Defoe, Wordsworth, Dickens, Pinter. I'd done *Romeo and Juliet* at school. My Dad's favourite book was *Robinson Crusoe*. I'd seen *Oliver* on the tele, but I'd never heard of Wordsworth, Pinter or Chaucer.

I began to shake. I couldn't do these. No way. Even if I could afford to buy them I couldn't study all these books. And that was just the literature list. There were three set texts for history that cost a bomb.

A giant, steely hand seemed to grab at my stomach. It squeezed hard and the force of the sudden pain made me double over. I staggered to my bed and lay down, rolled in a tight ball. I rocked myself backwards and forwards, backwards and forwards. My face was wet and sticky from tears and snot and I buried it in my pillow.

A Fresh Start

'You can do it Princess. You can do it.' My Dad's voice echoed in my head, but it seemed a long way off.

After a while I got up and washed my face, made some toast and a cup of tea. I collected my bag and my book lists and half an hour later I was in the Central Library looking for the books on the lists. I found *A Journal of The Plague Year*, *Hard Times* and *The Caretaker*. I'd also struck lucky with the history books. *The Making of the English Working Classes* and *The First Industrial Nation* weighed a ton, but I didn't care. As I hauled my bag onto my shoulder I felt a tingle of pride. Just carrying the books made me feel good. I felt as though I'd joined a special club. I was a student: an A level student.

When I got back to my place I put the books on the windowsill; arranged the literature books in alphabetical order, according to author; tagged the history ones onto the end of the row and stood back to admire my collection. It wasn't right. I rearranged the literature books chronologically; went out of the room; returned and glanced casually at the stack of books. My mouth dragged into a huge grin.

I walked across to my library, made a selection, sat on my bed and started to read.

*

Our first tests were in January. I'd done as much revision as possible over Christmas. I'd seen my Dad on Boxing Day and he'd said, 'I'm proud of you Princess. You'll do well. I know you will.' My Mum said, 'If you spent more time working at Sainsbury's and less time with your nose in a book you'd be better off.'

I was shivering with cold and nerves as I took my place at the back of the classroom. The room was freezing. We were on the side of the building that was shaded from the morning sun, the heating system was crap and the windows didn't shut properly. Mrs. Clarke gave out the test papers and my hand was shaking as I started to write.

The next four weeks were hell. I felt sure that what I'd written was shit. Then I convinced myself that I'd done well — I'd managed to answer all the questions and had finished all the essays. In lessons I looked for clues in the lecturer's face. She avoided my eyes. She looked at me pityingly. She looked at me with pleasure. By the time the papers had been marked I was cracking up.

'It's obvious, Lydia, that you've tried very hard,' she said, 'but I'm afraid you're just not ready for A levels yet. Maybe in a year or two when you've done your GCSEs. You shouldn't really have been accepted on this course.'

I didn't say anything. I felt stiff and cold. My brain seemed solid; frozen. I couldn't squeeze a thought from it. Blobs of wet splashed the folder I was hugging to my chest. Tears were streaming down my face and my nose was oozing. Mrs. Clarke handed me a tissue. I took it and scrunched it tightly in my hand. 'Wipe your face, Lydia.'

'My Dad said I could do A levels,' I said.

A Fresh Start

'You will do A levels, Lydia; just not yet, not now.'

'My Dad said I could do A levels.' I couldn't think of anything else to say. I couldn't stop my shoulders heaving. The tears poured faster and faster.

'It's all right Lydia,' she said, 'you can stay in the class until June. If your attendance improves and you get extra tuition from Open Learning, maybe that'll help. We'll assess the situation again in June.'

*

I cut my hours at Sainsbury's and just about managed to keep myself afloat. I spent all my free time in the library and increased my visits to my Mum's. I tried to avoid the times I knew slime-ball would be there, but I didn't always get it right. As soon as I saw him lounging in the big armchair — fat, gross and sweating — I backed out, pretending I'd forgotten something important. My Mum didn't seem to cotton on: she was just really pleased that I was making an effort to visit more often. I couldn't tell her I'd come because I was hungry.

I tried to hold on to fifty pence each week to phone my Dad. I needed to hear his voice: to hear him say, 'That's my girl. I'm proud of you Princess.'

*

'I thought you might like a coffee. Excuse me, I thought you might like a coffee.' I glanced up and Andy was holding two cups of coffee. 'Would you like a cup of coffee? he asked.

'I don't drink coffee,' I said.

'I can change it for tea.'
'I'm not thirsty,' I said.
'All right if I sit here?'
'It's a free country.'
'Do you really think so?'

We talked about history and literature; about film and art. We hung out at MAC, drinking in the bar and went to the occasional film. We walked in the park — glowing with the yellow and reds of daffodils and tulips.

When I could no longer pay my bills he talked his Mum and Dad into letting me crash out at their pad. Their house was big and rambling. 'A Victorian terrace with many of the original features,' his Mum said, looking pleased and smug. I was given the attic. Andy's old train set was laid out on a specially built platform, but there was still plenty of room for me and my gear. A single bed, where Andy's mates usually slept, stood underneath the skylight, a rickety chest of drawers next to it.

Each morning as the sun lit up a corner of the room I woke up smiling. I was studying A levels and I had Andy. It felt good — warm and soft and safe.

I didn't tell my Mum about my change of address. She wouldn't have liked me living with another family. But there was nothing she could do to help — not while slime-ball was still with her. I didn't tell my Dad either. It would have spoilt things for him, so I just didn't. I had to tell Biddy Baxter from social services. It would've caused too much hassle not to.

A Fresh Start

College was cool. I spent every spare minute in the library. I loved reading and studying my texts. I was actually looking forward to the end of year exams. We went to Stratford to see Kenneth Branagh in *Hamlet*. Andy bought my ticket: it was really, really cool.

*

'My Gran's coming to stay.' Andy frowned and he looked beyond me to the garden that was bursting with early summer colour. 'We'll be needing your room.'

'How long for?' I could feel sweat break out on my back, and then a great shiver made me shake from head to toe.

'She's sick. She's coming for good.'

There was no immediate rush. His Gran would be in hospital for at least a week and he'd help me find somewhere to live. I could increase my hours at Sainsbury's to pay my bills and I could still eat with them a couple of times a week.

His Mum said nothing when I saw her later that day though she looked at me with wide eyes full of pity. His Dad gave me a big hug, but he didn't say anything either. I hate people who do that.

*

It was cold and damp as I hurried away from Andy's house. I was scared. I'd never been out alone late at night. I wanted to call my Dad, but he wouldn't be there, not in the middle of the week. Anyway I couldn't tell him — I couldn't worry him. I couldn't tell my Mum either. She didn't even know I'd changed my address. I didn't have a plan. I just knew I couldn't stand Andy's Mum's cow-eyed pity and his Dad's stupid silence.

My rucksack was heavy. I was knackered and cold. I walked as fast as I could along the quiet, empty pavement, praying I wouldn't meet anyone. Even my eyeballs ached with sadness and loneliness, but I didn't cry.

The trees in Cannon Hill Park looked like huge, prehistoric monsters, lurking in the misty dark. As I heaved my rucksack onto the top of the gate I heard a car nearby. I panicked and let go my rucksack and it fell, with a loud wallop, into the park. I hesitated for a moment, but when a bright beam of light arched over the footbridge I ran to the darkest corner, my breath shallow and painful with fright. The car came on, and for a few terrifying seconds I thought the light would catch me, crouched like a frightened animal amongst the filth and rubbish, but it swung in a wide circle, drove back across the bridge and disappeared.

I waited a few moments, then raced to the gate and hurled myself over. Breathing hard, I walked towards the clump of bushes on the path to the left. I knew that behind the bushes was a secluded, sheltered spot, just big enough for two people to lie close together.

There was no moon and the mist that clung to the trees made the dark thick and spooky so it took ages to find my special place. I fumbled with my sleeping bag, spread it on the damp, rotten leaves and zipped myself in. I tucked my head right down and lay shivering with cold and terror, but I didn't cry.

A Fresh Start

'You're keen love,' the college receptionist said as I trudged past at eight o'clock next morning, sagging under the weight of my rucksack.

I went straight to the gym, slowly peeled the stiff clothes from my stinking body and stood in the shower for a long time until the piercing, hot water made my blood flow.

Andy didn't come to class that day, or for the rest of term. We were doing revision so I guessed he decided he could work better at home.

After the third night I didn't go back to the park. It was too scary. And it was crap when it rained. So I found my place under the stairs in the block of flats in Northfield. It was dark and damp and I couldn't stand upright because the ceiling sloped, but it was safe, and I could leave my things pushed into the far corner and know they wouldn't be pinched.

I showered at college and my Mum did my washing 'cause I said the washing machine at my place had broken, and when I wasn't working at Sainsbury's I stayed in the library or walked in the park.

*

It was steaming hot in the classroom. The desks were arranged in rows and everyone was talking and laughing really loudly. I sat down, closed my eyes and took deep breaths. I didn't want to see Andy. I didn't want to know where he was sitting. I just wanted to concentrate on the mock exam. If I did well I could progress to the second year.

Mrs. Clarke was handing out the papers when the door opened. I glanced up and saw Andy hesitate for a moment and then hurry towards the back of the room.

*

'I'm sorry Lydia, I have to recommend that you transfer to a full-time GCSE course. Your results are very poor, I'm afraid.'

The sun was dazzling and it was hot, but I couldn't stop shivering. A group of students stood together, laughing and shouting, shoving each other playfully, getting louder and louder. As I walked slowly past a young man fell backwards and knocked against my arm.

'Come for a drink with us, Lydia,' said Andy. 'We're all going down the Varsity to celebrate, come with us.'

The window behind him was ablaze with sunlight and his body was fuzzy and indistinct. I couldn't see his face.

I pushed past him and hurried away.

*

I'd shouted at Mrs. Clarke. I'd really lost it. 'You're ruining my life,' I screamed. 'You won't let me do what I want to do. You're a spiteful, old bitch. You've never liked me. You have a grudge against me. You're ruining my life. I have to do my A levels,' I screamed. 'I have to do my A levels. My Dad said I can do A levels.'

A Fresh Start

Mrs. Clarke looked shocked: frightened almost. When I started to sob, to slobber all over her folders, she'd put her arm around my shoulders and made soothing noises, but I shrugged her off and screamed, 'You spiteful bitch!'

I remember her face was white and frozen; her eyes round and startled.

*

I woke with a jolt in the pitch-black space. For a split second I lay stiff and cold, unable to remember where I was. Suddenly, the silence was broken and a thunderous noise came from just above my head followed by raised voices and squeals of laughter. The local kids were using the hall and staircase as a playground so it was probably raining outside.

I forced myself to stay put until the kids got bored and buggered off. Then I pushed the heavy door open a few inches and let in a slit of grey light. I found my rucksack, unpicked two slugs that clung to the webbing, crunched them with my doc martins and packed my sleeping bag.

The sleep had cleared my head. There was no point in playing the drama queen (I hate people who do that) and leaving everything behind on the off-chance that someone, sometime in the future, might find my stuff and imagine I'd been murdered or sold as a sex-slave. Naw, I'd take it with me.

I'd head for London. I was sure I could hitch a ride. I'd heard girls at college say they did it all the time. They were dozens of colleges in London and it was easy to get a job there and I could doss down in the parks until I found my own place.

I wouldn't tell my Mum and Dad just yet. I'd wait until I was sorted: until I'd made a fresh start.

Cold Comfort

'VILL-AAA, VILL-AAA, VILL-AAA, VILL-AAA; VILL-AAA; VILL-AAA, VILL-AAAAAA! The ferocity of the roar circling Villa Park almost flattened her as she hurried up the steps to take her seat in the lower Holt End. Thirty-four thousand throats opened and thirty-four thousand voices bellowed support for their team. This great swell of sound, bellicose and hectoring, was underscored by a yearning that stripped the nerves raw.

Emily, struggling to her seat, was almost decapitated by the less dilatory fans who rose as one to admonish the referee. 'FUCKIN' WANKER! GET YOUR BLEEDIN' EYES TESTED!'

'Ah well, the football may be crap but the wit's great,' she greeted her friend, Jean. 'Sorry I'm late: Pete's playing up again. What have I missed?'

'Nothing much — Southgate scored a penalty and Merson outpaced Shearer down the right-hand side — apart from that the first minutes of the game were uneventful.'

'Merson's not even on the pitch.'

'Trust you to quibble.'

'STAND UP IF YOU LOVE VILL-AAA. STAND UP IF YOU LOVE VILL-AAA.' Always a bit reluctant to declare undying love for eleven men simultaneously, and in public, Emily and Jean nevertheless jumped to their feet. They had little choice if they wanted to follow the progress of the match. Young men of every shape and size, draped in Villa colours, the most unbecoming woolly hats in the entire world perched precariously on shaven heads, arms stretched skywards, paid homage to their team and blocked the view of the less zealous. Then, temporarily becalmed by their outpouring of affection, the fans sat down once again.

Most of the play was taking place at the North End where Villa mounted attack after futile attack on the Newcastle goal. It was difficult from the Holt End to really make sense of what was happening unless you kept an eye on the giant screens. Emily knew that these screens had a perfectly rational function — they allowed spectators to choose whether to concentrate on the hurly-blurry of the pitch action or to have a clear view of play, but she hated them. She came to a football match to see live action: if she wanted to look at football on television she'd stay at home. The fact that she had neither Sky Sport nor cable and that Pete wouldn't allow her to watch *Match of the Day* didn't deter her from clinging to her rather irrational position.

*

At the other end of the pitch streaks of claret and blue engaged in a frantic dance with black and white stripes. The player with the ball swayed tantalisingly, sold his marker a dummy, raced past him and with a wide-open goal to his left back-heeled the ball to

Wrighty on his right, (there was no mistaking the tiny speck that was Wrighty) who caught it on his chest, brought it down, did an eighty degrees turn to ward off an attacking Newcastle player, turned again and struck the ball hard and soundly towards the goal where Shay Given snatched it and held it lovingly to his breast.

'KICK THE FUCKIN' BALL! TIME WASTER. TIME WASTER.' The man directly in front of Emily was clearly unimpressed by the Newcastle goalie's prowess. A thundering shot from Given sent twenty players racing towards Villa's goal. The spectators in the Holt End jumped in unison to their feet. Clapping their hands, and then spreading them up and out, as though pleading with the ultimate football deity, they bellowed their frustration. 'SAME (clap) OLD (clap) GEORDIES (clap) ALWAYS CHEATING (arms outstretched). SAME OLD GEORDIES ALWAYS CHEATING. SAME OLD GEORDIES ALWAYS CHEATING.'

'What happened, what did Newcastle do?' Emily was perplexed.

'They wouldn't let diddums have the ball,' explained Jean.

'What? I don't ...' Emily's reply was lost in the tidal wave of anger that erupted on all sides. Near the touchline to her left a Villa player lay writhing in agony, his knees bent to his chest. The Newcastle player who'd brought him down stood a little way off, hands on hips, uncertain what to do. After a moment's thought he approached the injured Hendrie and gently touched his shoulder in apology.

'BASTARD! IT'S TOO LATE NOW YOU FUCKIN' WANKER. BASTARD! SEND HIM OFF REF. SEND THE WANKER OFF.'

Hendrie made no attempt to get to his feet. He continued to lie on the cold, winter grass, his face shrunken in pain. In a blizzard of activity, trainers and stretcher-bearers descended on him, talked to him, touched him carefully, talked to him again, lifted him gently onto a stretcher and carried him from the pitch.

A lone, plaintive cry came from the upper Holt End. It was taken up by other voices and developed into a howl of bitterness as it reverberated around the stadium, finally finding expression in a roar of anger.

'YOU'RE A FUCKIN' WANKER KETSBAIA. SEND HIM OFF REF. SEND HIM BACK TO RUSSIA.' This outburst was followed by a ripple of sympathetic applause as the Villa supporters acknowledged the departure of Hendrie.

'That poor bloke looked to be in terrible pain,' Emily turned to Jean, her face etched with worry and concern.

'He's a professional footballer, that's what he gets paid for.'

'I don't think you should come to football matches, you're being coarsened by the experience,' said Emily and then realized that her comment was almost a direct quote from Pete; almost the exact words he'd shouted at her as she'd slammed the door on leaving the house.

Cold Comfort

The Villa players continued to mount unsuccessful attacks on Newcastle's goal. Repeated failure added a desperation to their attempts which ensured repeated failure. To make matters worse the sharp, bright, winter sun disappeared, the startlingly-blue sky darkened to a filthy grey and sheets of cold, slanting rain blew vindictively in the direction of Villa's most ardent fans.

Emily's long, warm coat — a sensible choice in the clear crispness of the early afternoon — soaked up the rain like a thirsty sponge. Her bright-yellow, woollen cowl did little to protect her hair from the damp onslaught. Her leather gloves became wet and hard as the merciless rain was driven in her direction by a slicing wind. And there was little on the pitch to get excited about. Emily cursed silently: if Pete wasn't such a berk, so determined to tell her what to do, she'd be at home now, warm and cosy, reading her book, instead of catching her death at the Holt End.

*

Villa had most of the ball. They swayed and sallied, ran and swerved as the Newcastle players attempted, desperately, to gain possession. But time after depressing time, all efforts were wasted by Villa's lack of courage and conviction when it really mattered. They were incapable of getting the ball past Given. They were marking Shearer out of the game and still they couldn't score.

It was all too much for the man seated directly behind Emily. He found an outlet for his disgust by venting his spleen on his own team. 'Don't tackle him Wrighty,' he urged, 'he's expecting that — surprise him, let him pass. Atta-a-boy! It's behind ya, Taylor. Behind ya. That big space with the net — it's called a goal.'

Once Motormouth had started he couldn't seem to shut up. Wet and cold, and bored with the match Emily tuned in and enjoyed his nonsense. When he'd finished taunting the players he chose his targets at random. 'The fleecies are out in full today. They'll be waterlogged before half-time. Won't be able to lift themselves off the seats. Serve them right. Baaa! Baaa! It's time we clubbed together and bought Merson a zimmer frame. Hey! Did ya hear about Barry Strutter? Ya know he was done for fancying kids or something like that? Well, apparently his bird blew him out. She said, 'I can't go out with you anymore because you're a paedophile.' And Barry said, 'That's a very big word for an eight year-old.'

*

'I can't understand why you want to go to football matches,' Pete said, time and again. He'd never liked football and couldn't see its appeal, especially for a woman. In an attempt to convert him, to introduce him to the excitement and pleasure of the experience, Emily made the mistake of persuading him to join her and Jean one Sunday afternoon. He'd been appalled at the level of vulgarity and what he called 'the repressed violence' that swirled around the stadium. 'This is no place for a respectable woman,' he'd said.

Cold Comfort

And Emily had laughed. She was sure he was joking. But his stony expression told her she was mistaken.

*

Emily was nudged on her left side. 'Here, have a swig of this, it'll keep the blood flowing.' Surreptitiously, Jean handed her a small, silver flask. She threw back her head and attempted to clasp the neck between her chattering teeth and, at the same time, swallow a hefty measure. She felt the smooth liquid warm her throat, chest and belly. Then she thought of Pete's reaction if he saw her glugging whisky on the football terraces and she was racked by a hacking cough. 'Serves you right for being such a greedy pig,' was Jean's unsympathetic response to Emily's difficulties. Unable to catch her breath and with tears streaming down her face, she was momentarily powerless before her friend's cruelty. Wheezing and gasping she eventually managed to splutter, 'Don't think I'll forget this. I'll never come to another match with you — you're uncouth.' Dear, god, she thought, I'm sounding more and more like Prissy Pete.

*

Thankfully, the referee blew the half-time whistle. Her bones crackling from the cold and damp, Emily followed Jean down the steps and into the shelter of the vast, bleak foyer. There was a long, straggling queue at every refreshment counter. 'I'd kill for a decent cup of hot tea and something nice to eat,' said Emily.

'You could commit mass-murder and you still wouldn't get your wish — the stuff they serve here is disgusting,' snapped Jean.

'Just because the team is useless, there's no need to take it out on me,' Emily retorted.

'The team is NOT useless. We've had most of the play. Newcastle's not getting a look in. It's only a matter of time before we score. You're so bleedin' negative.' Emily had reached the counter so she didn't bother to reply. When she'd been served she clasped the plastic container of scalding tea in her numbed hands. Slowly, the heat penetrated her sodden gloves and her fingers began to tingle.

She looked for a place among the heaving crush where she could stand and drink the hot, greasy liquid. Thousands of women, men and children were jammed together, glad to be out of the freezing rain. There was not an inch of space, so she had to go where she was pushed. Monitors, hanging like giant, frozen birds from the ceiling, offered some distraction from the grim reality. Those close enough to see, voiced their frustration as the progress of the day's other matches was relayed. The mention of Manchester United called forth a blistering torrent of abuse. The news that Leeds was doing well was met by a resounding cheer. 'How come they're so fond of Leeds all of a sudden?' asked Emily.

'Because Leeds are challenging Man United at the top of the league, stupid. I don't know why you call yourself a football enthusiast, you know nothing about the game,' snorted Jean.

Cold Comfort

'As a Villa enthusiast I'd be much more impressed if *they* were challenging Man United at the top of the league,' she snapped back. But Jean's remark had stung. She knew she didn't really understand the finer points of the game: if she lived to be a hundred she'd never grasp the off-side rule, but she genuinely enjoyed the element of theatre that a football match involved — the excruciating tension, the high drama. If only Pete would stop going on, would quit putting pressure on her to give it up, she'd limit her attendance and the novelty value would ensure that she enjoyed the experience once again. But he wouldn't leave it alone.

And now he'd started on about the way she dressed — 'too tarty', he said.

They followed the undulating mass of claret and blue back to the stand. Emily shivered when she saw the lashing rain, metallic and icy, reflected in the floodlights. The second half had better be good.

*

The teams raced onto the pitch and the young bloods stood, arms outstretched, heralding the return of 'VILLA'S CLARET AND BLUE ARMY VILLA'S CLARET AND BLUE ARMY.' Once again the stadium was engulfed in a great wave of sound as thousands of spectators urged their team 'TO GET STUCK IN; TO CUT THE CRAP; TO PLAY FUCKIN' FOOTBALL; TO STOP PRATTING ABOUT; TO SCORE A FUCKIN'GOAL.'

As the torrent of vulgarity poured down as vehemently as the rain, Emily wondered if Pete was right: perhaps football stadiums were brutal places, unfit for women and children. She glanced round her. The women and children scattered liberally among the predominantly male crowd showed no signs of distress; they were shouting and pointing, urging their team on. But, the thought struck her, that's exactly Pete's point — according to him we're all being coarsened by our participation.

*

Villa was attacking the Holt End and the fans supported them with all the lungpower at their disposal. Each sally on the Newcastle goal was accompanied by the crowd, acting as one, jumping to their feet and bellowing their encouragement, advice and criticism in a paroxysm of longing. With all the strength they possessed they willed their team to score.

Sixty-five minutes into the match, disaster struck. Ketsbaia, the demon of the first half who'd caused Hendrie's injury, sent a soaring cross in the direction of Duncan Ferguson. Ferguson was still trying to get his bearings, having been on the pitch a mere seven minutes. However, Villa's defence, apparently taking leave of their senses as well of the goal area, allowed the veteran Newcastle player to pop one into the back of the net.

'YEEEEESSS!' THE North End exploded with a mighty cheer. The Newcastle crowd went wild with delight. They leapt to their feet, arms aloft, punching the air. They hugged each other, shouted, danced and sang. From where Emily and Jean were standing it looked as though thousands of Geordie fans were playing on a giant bouncy-castle.

A deathly silence descended on the Holt End. Villa supporters could not believe their eyes. It wasn't fair. They'd had most of the play. They'd had most of the chances. Their players had worked harder. Villa had been guilty of just one lapse in vigilance and that rotten, geriatric Ferguson had put one away. It wasn't fair.

Hoots of derision were flung at them from the far end of the pitch. The Newcastle supporters stood, right arms outstretched, index fingers stabbing the gloom, bellowing with all their might. 'YOU'RE *CRAP* AND YOU KNOW IT. YOU'RE *SHIT* AND YOU KNOW IT. *YOU'RE* NOT SINGING ANYMORE. *YOU'RE* NOT SINGING ANYMORE.'

*

Villa fans did their best to rally their team as they once again bombarded the Newcastle goal. 'COME ON VILLA. COME ON VILLA. SHOOT. SHOOT. KICK THE FUCKIN' BALL.'

Every time the ball came towards them everyone in the Holt End jumped to their feet, shouting, chanting, screaming, urging the players to do that one simple thing — SCORE A GOAL.

'Dear lord,' Emily's hoarse shout was almost drowned by the cacophony of sound, 'I don't know why I allow you to talk me into paying to endure this torture. I must be insane.'

'Shut yer gob and support your team,' yelled Jean.

By now completely demoralized, Motormouth once again got his tongue into gear. 'Attaboy, Southgate,' he roared, 'you just stand there, don't you go tackling those ruffians, you might get hurt.'

The man standing next to Emily could endure no more. He'd remained strangely taciturn throughout the match, but the sarcasm of one of his own goaded him to retort. His face ashen from both cold and tension, he gave voice to his pent up emotions.

'I'm suffering from a surfeit of cynicism,' he hissed. 'I don't know why people come to football matches if they only have negative things to say about their own players.' He glared over his shoulder at the unabashed derider of his team.

Emily tugged at Jean's sleeve. 'I think your man next to me is a bit weird.' she said, 'Can I change places with you?'

'Shut your gob and support your team,' shouted Jean.

'Is that all you can say? Is that the extent of your response, the extent of your vocabulary?'

'For god's sake they nearly scored. Did you see that? Did you see that pass from Wrighty? Merson nearly scored.'

'Nearly is just not good enough.' said Emily, huffily.

'I'm with you there, love.' Motormouth touched Emily's shoulder in solidarity.

'You can piss off and all,' she snapped.

Cold Comfort

Pete was right: she had become a mouthy, vulgar cow. Standing on the terraces she shouted, roared, used language she wouldn't use elsewhere. She jumped up and down, pointed, snapped at people. But this behaviour didn't terrify her as it did him. For her it was a healthy way to let off steam. Each week thousands of people who lived cheek by jowl in cities, streamed into football stadiums, brought together by their allegiance to their local team (with the exception of Man United of course) and found a release for all the pressures and stresses of their daily lives. She thought that was good and, for the most part, harmless. Pete didn't. She was prepared to agree to differ. He wasn't. What if he couldn't? The thought chilled her. What if he wouldn't or couldn't see her point of view in any of their areas of disagreement? What if those areas of disagreement increased and multiplied? At the moment it was football, the way she dressed. What might he pick on next?

*

Unable to endure the pain of seeing her team fail to capitalize on their numerous sorties on Newcastle's goal and not wanting to think about herself and Pete, Emily looked for distraction. At the far end of the pitch she could see bright patches of yellow mingling with the Geordie supporters. Excitedly, she poked Jean in the ribs. 'There's a fight down the other end. Look, there are dozens of coppers. But why would they argue amongst themselves when their team's winning?'

'What? What are you talking about?' asked Jean, exasperated at being distracted in the final minutes of the game.

'Look, the police are breaking up a fight at the other end.'

'Why would they fight each other, especially when they're winning?'

'Because northerners are inherently violent?'

'If I thought for one minute you were serious I'd start a fight down this end. You are one stupid tart! The police are mingling with the supporters because the match is almost finished and they're waiting to escort them from the stadium. Now shut the fuck up. Villa might still pull one back.'

A sharp, piercing sound shrilled high and wide. The struggle was over. Villa had lost.

*

The crowd started the weary trudge home; they shuffled slowly and disconsolately from the stadium. The evening sky had been washed clean by the heavy rain that had finally stopped. The wind was cold and harsh against the skin. 'That was a load of crap. Imagine spending eighteen pounds to watch a load of crap like that and to get soaked and frozen into the bargain — and when you think of the money that lot get paid!'

'Ah, shut yer gob. Be thankful you're not a season-ticket holder.' Jean was not in the mood to listen to her friend's griping.

'Yeah, I suppose things can only get better. This time last year we were top of the league. Maybe they'll turn things round.'

'Yeah, and maybe Man United will commit collective hara kiri.'

Jean linked arms with Emily. 'Sorry for being such a grump,' she said. It was a nerve-racking game. But apart from their inability to find the goal, they played well.'

'Jean', Emily said.

'Yeah.'

'If I needed to, could I ... could I come and stay at yours for a while?' Jean's eyebrows disappeared into her hairline, but she didn't miss a beat with her reply.

'Of course you can,' she said, linking arms, and then added, 'Hey, do you fancy a Balti?'

'That sounds good,' said Emily.

*

All round them thousands of fans hurried out of the winter chill. Hundreds of cars started up, sending exhaust fumes billowing into the dark. Snippets of conversation frosted the evening air.

'That Ketsba ... what's his name ... should be banned for life.'

'I could murder a fry-up, I could. The works — bacon, sausage, tomatoes, eggs, beans, mushrooms, all swimming in hot grease.'

'Uuugh! You're disgusting.'

'That ref was a wanker. He needed his eyes testing.'

'Dad, what's a wanker?'

'I think they should wear the away strip at home, the colour is more flattering.'

'They're on the up. They only conceded one goal. That's not bad, considering.'

'THERE'S ONLY ONE ASTON VILLA! THERE'S ONLY ONE ASTON VILLA! THERE'S ONLY ONE ASTON VILLA!

'One's bleedin' enough, that's what I say.'

Something to Tell

'It eez verry cold, Costin. You mast wrrap ap verry warm.' His mother's voice exuded maternal concern and his heart cramped with pain, but he laughed his reply.

'An English winter is like a Romanian spring, Mama. I won't be cold.' A wisp of sadness drifted across his mother's face and she turned away. He cursed silently. He'd taken great care over the past week to avoid all mention of home and had succeeded until now.

'Heve a gud time with yerr frriends, Costin. You must tell me everrything tomorrow.'

He shivered as he waited for the lift on the dim, smelly landing. Despite his assurances to his mother he suffered greatly from the English winters. The cold and damp crept into his bones and stayed in residence until summer.

It was his third winter in England and each year he'd assumed it would get better, but it didn't.

*

He emerged from the tall, grey block of flats into the crisp night air. Hesitating for a moment, he wrapped his scarf tightly around his neck and pulled his hood into place. Fuck that crap about Romanian springs — it was fuckin' freezing and he had nowhere to go. In

GILDED SHADOWS

the yellow glow of a street light he glanced at his watch. It was half-past eight. He couldn't return home until after mid-night so he had at least four hours to kill on New Year's Eve in a city full of strangers.

He crossed the road, took a right onto the Bristol Road, and walked briskly towards the city centre. It would take nearly two hours to reach Holloway Circus, and then what?

*

His footsteps beat out a steady rhythm on the frosty pavement. Cars sped by with an harmonious swish. The rest was silence. The deserted streets intensified his feeling of isolation. He could have stayed in the flat with his mother and welcomed the New Year in with her, but she'd been so eager for him to go out, to enjoy himself, for him to be with his 'Eengleesh frriends'.

On his left the lights from the Orthopaedic Hospital beckoned, warm and welcoming. He imagined the patients inside, tucked up in bed, secure and happy in the knowledge that they weren't alone, that there was someone to care for them. Hospital seemed a good place to be at this time of year. Maybe he should have pushed his mother down the lift-shaft and thrown himself after her.

He raised his chin from his chest and looked around. Still no one. It was really spooky. He was walking along one of the busiest roads in a city of a million people and he was the only one to be seen. Actually, that was wrong. As he didn't have a mirror

Something to Tell

he couldn't actually be seen — unless there was someone lurking in the shadows, observing him in silence.

Hurriedly, he crossed to the other side of the road and was confronted by the college he attended four days a week. It rose, dark and gloomy, behind the emaciated trees that screened it from the Bristol Road. His feeling of unease increased so he tucked his chin into his collar and quickened his pace.

College was the brightest spot in his life and he hated the holidays. All his fellow students seemed to look forward to the break from lessons and homework: they welcomed the prospect of staying at home with their families and the extra opportunities to socialise. For him, the vacations were black holes where he lost all sense of purpose, all sense of self.

After his early–morning paper round he was forced to spend most of the day in the flat with his mother. The longing in her eyes, the sadness that enveloped her, her insistence on speaking a fractured English — all of these he found unbearable, so he escaped to his room and spent hours in front of the computer. Occasionally, as the flat closed in round him, he was forced out to wander the streets.

*

Keeping his head down against the bitter night air, he trudged on through the deserted suburbs. As he stepped off the pavement at Witherford Way, the sound of screeching brakes startled him out of his reverie. He raised his hand in apology to the angry driver. If he wasn't careful he wouldn't live to tell his mother about the riotous evening he'd spent in the company of dozens of 'Eengleesh frriends'.

He passed Selly Oak Colleges and at last he spotted another pedestrian. He was not the last inhabitant of a post-holocaust planet after all. Sukbinder would be glad to hear it. Or maybe he'd be disappointed. You could never tell with that little weirdo: a bloke of seventeen who was a *Star Wars* freak was difficult to figure out. 'Darvada is bril,' he'd said to Costin as they sat in the canteen in no hurry to return to class. Costin had thought he was speaking a foreign language. 'I do not understand,' he'd replied. 'Have yow niver hird of *Star Wars?*' Sukbinder was incredulous, and he proceeded to deliver a lecture on the *Star Wars* phenomenon that lasted half an hour. Costin understood little of what was said, they were twenty-five minutes late for GCSE English, they received a tongue-lashing from Mrs. Griffin, but he had made his first English friend.

*

By the time he'd reached the junction of Oak Tree Lane the pavements were liberally sprinkled with groups of young people. Their voices rang out loud and cackling in the frosty air. To combat the cold they nestled warmly together, arms linked, companionable and cosy. Costin quickly averted his gaze as he approached each group.

To comfort himself he directed his thoughts to his friend. Sukbinder was spherical. He had a round head

Something to Tell

that sat on top of a short, round body with little neck to speak of. The overall impression was of something formless and squidgy. Costin constantly fought an urge to grab handfuls of Sukbinder's soft flesh. He worried about this desire, worried that he might have what his mother considered 'unnaturrral errrges which only people in the West are prone to,' until he realized that what Sukbinder had in abundance was baby-appeal. Costin wondered whether Sukbinder's obsession with planets had its subliminal trigger in his own shape.

*

The pubs in Selly Oak throbbed to the sounds of revelry. Although it was not yet half past nine hundreds of people were crammed together, shouting and laughing above loud, thumping music. Despite his best efforts Costin's gaze was drawn towards the glowing lights. The windows framed a scene of festive enjoyment and he was unable to quell the longing to be part of it.

As he opened the door of the pub he was enveloped in a warm, damp blanket of air. It took him ten minutes to fight his way to the bar, but he didn't mind. He enjoyed the bodily contact that was inevitable in the crowded room. Apart from his mother, it had been a long time since he'd come this close to another person and it was a good feeling. Twenty minutes later he finally gave his order for half a pint of lager, but he didn't mind that it had taken so long.

Being part of the mass of young, heaving, noisy bodies was good.

'Hi ya Cos! What yow doin' mate?' The greeting was accompanied by a slap to his right shoulder and he spilt a large dollop of lager over the young woman standing next to him, but she didn't seem to notice. Kevin from GCSE Biology waved a twenty-pound note in Costin's direction. 'Get's a round mate. Yow 'ave one. We're over 'ere in the corner.'

It was next to impossible to manoeuvre the tray of beer through the packed room, but somehow he made it with the drinks more or less intact. 'Where yow off to mate?' Kevin shouted, trying to make himself heard above the din.

'I am going into town,' Costin yelled.

'Yow gowing to meet some mates?' roared Kevin. Costin smiled his reply.

'We've stopped off 'ere for a few bevies, loike, and then we're off to a party,' Kevin was hoarse with the effort of making himself heard. 'Pity yows fixed up or yow could've come along.'

Half an hour later Costin found himself, once again, walking through the cold, winter night towards the city centre. He'd left the pub with Kevin and his mates. He didn't feel inclined to linger alone. On the pavement outside they'd slapped him good-naturedly on the back and shouted loudly and vulgarly as he waved goodbye, a smile fixed to his frozen face.

*

Something to Tell

It was twenty-five past eleven when he reached Holloway Circus. Groups of people were walking or rushing in every direction. Taxis swished by or stopped to disgorge their drunken passengers. Everywhere the mood was jovial and happy. The undercurrent of hostility and fear that usually tainted the city after dark had disappeared. People seemed relaxed and friendly. It was New Year's Eve and differences were forgotten. All round him families and friends walked by, happy to be together on this special night.

He allowed himself to be swept along by the tide of people heading towards Centenary Square. He checked for traffic before crossing Severn Street and his heart thumped with pleasure. That was Allen — just ahead of him. Allen was his other special friend from college who had casually mentioned that he might be in town on New Year's Eve. Although he knew the chances of meeting him in a crowd of sixty thousand revellers were less than slim, it was that slim chance that had kept Costin going during the long trek into town. He couldn't believe his luck. Allen was there — just a couple of yards away.

*

'Do you know what to do?' Allen had asked him when they'd been instructed to work in pairs and to underline examples of figurative language in a passage of prose. Costin had understood the requirements of the task, but identifying metaphor and simile in English was beyond him. Allen and he had sat in a haze of confusion during the twenty minutes allotted to the task.

Newly arrived from Kenya, Allen was alone and lonely in Birmingham, and was glad to tag along with Costin and Sukbinder. They made an unusual trio: the tall, handsome, well-built African; the soft, round, fat Asian; the thin, pale-faced Romanian with their individual obsessions — body-building, inter-galactic warfare and computers. Within the college they became inseparable, meeting during break and for lunch. They found they had one particular interest in common — poker — and they spent every spare minute in the canteen indulging their passion.

They were frequently late for class and their work and their relationships with lecturers suffered as a result. But they didn't care. An egalitarian loneliness bound them together and an occasional bollocking from a lecturer was a small price to pay for the comfort they found in each other's company.

Although Costin longed for it with all his heart their friendship didn't function beyond the college. Sukbinder's journey home took about two hours and when he arrived a large family, whom he hated with an uncharacteristic ferocity, was waiting for him. Discouraged from making friends outside his cultural group he took refuge in his room and fought his silent wars as a substitute for the familial battle he desperately wanted to wage. Allen, the oldest of the three, the most street-wise and the one with most money, tended to spend his spare time in the gym or clubbing in the city centre. Costin went home, reluctantly, to his bleak flat where he watched television with his mother or sat in front of his computer until the small hours.

Many times he'd been on the verge of suggesting a meeting in town to see a film or to hang out, but at the last minute he always lost courage, afraid his friends would read in his voice the depths of his loneliness.

*

In a frantic attempt to reach Allen he pushed his way through the crush of people. He called out, but his voice was lost in the squeals of enjoyment reverberating round the festive streets of Birmingham. In his hurry he tripped over the wheels of a pushchair and as he struggled to stay upright, was forced to take his eyes off his friend. When he looked again Allen had gone.

By now the crowd had reached Holliday Street and was fanning out onto the Queensway. It felt good to take command of the normally busy road where cars usually sped by, their occupants intent on getting to their destination unhindered by human contact. It felt good to be part of such an enormous gathering, to be with people of all ages, to be alongside men, women and children from the diverse ethnic groups which Birmingham was home to.

'Yow all roight bab? Didn't hurt yow did Oi?' The woman with the pushchair bellowed to make herself heard.

'I am fine, thank you,' Costin shouted.

'Here, yow have one of these bab.' Plunging her hand into the bag that hung from the pushchair she offered Costin a can of beer. Costin smiled and shouted his thanks.

*

Having reached the top of Broad Street the crowd was forced to a standstill as it joined the revellers already cramming the area. Costin squeezed his skinny frame through the mass of bodies, bent his supple limbs around barriers, dodged the stewards and found a spot in Centenary Square.

On the gigantic stage a group of young musicians entertained the crowds with great enthusiasm. The music was loud. The raw, sexy twang of the guitar and the deep, resonant throb of the bass were almost obliterated by the frantic clamouring of the drums. The vocalist screamed herself hoarse, afraid she might not be heard.

All round was good humour and laughter. It was New Year's Eve, Centenary Square was ablaze with light and festivity and the people of Birmingham were determined to make the most of it.

As the countdown to the New Year began Costin clambered onto a wall to get a better view.

He was suffused with delight at the scene before him. Again and again fireworks shot towards the heavens, exploded with a shock of sound and drenched the sky in a rainbow of colours. The excitement of the night sky was reflected in the square. At each burst of sound and colour the crowd

Something to Tell

sent up a mighty cheer. The haloes of flickering light worn by thousands of children and teenagers bounced — green, red, yellow and blue — in a kaleidoscopic frenzy around the huge space.

Costin gave himself up to the rumbustious excitement of it all. His voice joined the sixty thousand others as they shouted their welcome to the New Year. He returned the embrace of the drunk standing, rather unsteadily, next to him. He raised his arms and swayed from side to side singing, who knows what? His face stretched into a beaming smile.

*

At first Costin thought it was raining. He felt spots of moisture on his cheeks. Gradually the spots blended together and flowed downwards, running off his chin and splashing onto his scarf. A rasping sob jumped from his mouth and his shoulders started to shake. The expression on his face was a mixture of surprise and helplessness. Again and again he wiped his eyes with the back of his hand, but the tears continued to flow.

*

The blow hit him low and hard. His knees buckled and he lost his balance. Trying desperately to steady himself he grabbed for the drunk and caught hold of his arm. For a few brief seconds they swayed precariously in a bizarre dance before falling to the ground.

Shaken and bruised Costin lay next to his inebriated companion on the cold concrete. He looked towards the winter sky and into the face of a smiling Allen who stood assured and confident on the narrow ledge from which Costin had fallen.

'You're a wimp, man,' Allen shouted. 'I pat you on the back and you fall to the ground like a girl. Get up here.'

Costin jumped to his feet. He dragged the drunk upright, propped him against the ledge and clambered up beside his friend. 'I'm going to gatecrash a party, man, do you want to come?'

Costin wasn't quite sure what gatecrash meant but whatever it was he wanted to be part of it. He nodded his assent and followed Allen's muscular figure as he pushed his way through the crowd.

A smile of happiness spread across Costin's thin, pale face. His mother would be pleased. He would have something to tell her. In fact, he would keep her happy for weeks, telling her about the New Year's party he'd been to with his English friend.

Aftermath

'One brief moment can change our lives dramatically,' the breathy voice of the presenter confided. 'In our programme today we will be talking to people who were going about their everyday lives when they had an experience, the aftermath of which changed them completely.' Invariably the poor sods who'd agreed to bare their souls for the delectation of bored housewives had been rendered helpless by the vagaries of fate. One unfortunate woman had come home early from work to find her new husband in bed with her teenage son and, surprise, surprise, that moment of discovery had changed her life forever.

Why anyone would want to share her private travails with the whole nation was beyond Anne. She had no wish to hear a repeat of the programme she'd listened to, with increasing exasperation, earlier that day so she leaned forward and switched to Radio Three.

*

She'd dithered about leaving the comfort of John's flat and returning to her empty house, but now that she'd left the gloomy, residential roads of Moseley behind, she was pleased with her decision. The lure of her own bed had been too great to resist. The familiarity of its firm mattress, soft pillow and goose-down duvet had beckoned and she'd said, 'Yeah.' Of course if she gave in to John's pleas and moved in with him she wouldn't have to grapple constantly with the decision of whether to stay or go. Her daughters thought she was mad not to jump at the chance. 'He is soooo hot, Mum,' they squealed, 'go for it.' She knew their slightly hysterical excitement hid the real fear they felt about her living alone. They'd been over-protective since the death of their father: feared she might be burgled: have an accident or die alone. They didn't give voice to what they dreaded most, but she could read it in the unfinished sentence; in the words left hanging in the air.

The children had turned into the parent: they wanted to see her happy and settled. She also knew their urgings were tinged with self-interest. If she wasn't alone Sue would feel better about setting off on her world travels and Clare wouldn't feel compelled to ring her and visit her so often to check that she'd made it through the night.

But twenty-five years of family life, of putting everyone else's needs before hers had left their mark. She'd done it willingly, loved almost every minute. But in the aftermath of Mark's death, when the pain and emptiness had subsided, she discovered, somewhat guiltily, that she enjoyed being a singleton: enjoyed the freedom to please herself and the confidence that came with making her own decisions.

*

Aftermath

The night was cold and clear. There was a new moon and even some stars. Despite all the dire warnings about the vulnerability of lone women driving at night, she was enjoying the journey. She snuggled into her seat and paid attention to the music that soared from the radio. Holst's *Jupiter* filled the enclosed space and her spirits lifted as the music reached its joyful finale. She reached over and flicked the central-locking device to open. Sod the scaremongers. She would not be cowed in her own city.

The landmarks along the way were comfortingly familiar. To her left Moseley Baths squatted low and shabby, bowed by years of neglect. Through a couple of roundabouts, and St. Andrews loomed, a monument of vulgarity to the beautiful game. She smiled as she visualized the thousands of fans who converged on the stadium, full of expectation, throughout the season. They emerged in rivulets from the surrounding roads then joined together in a rushing swell that emptied into the vast tunnels leading to the pitch — part of the great wave of humanity that breathed energy and life into the city.

*

Soon she'd be in a warm bath, she'd have a night-cap and then abandon herself to the comfort of her bed with Bill Bryson's *The Lost Continent*. It was a good laugh. It hadn't been her choice for the book club and it certainly wasn't 'great literature', but it was good bedtime reading: undisturbing and relaxing.

The roads were quiet in this area: a stray car here and there, but nothing more. The city was relaxing into the peace of the night. It had untied its belt, thrown off its shoes and sighed with relief that the hustle and bustle of the day had ended.

Her foot pressed lightly on the brake as she prepared to turn into Belcher's Lane, then the sound of raised voices, muffled but aggressive, penetrated her safe haven.

Six teenage lads ran recklessly across the road. One had broken away from the group and was toiling to maintain his lead. Shouts of, 'Get him, get the bastard,' reached her. She felt a cramp of anxiety under her left breast.

The engine stalled and her left hand automatically sought the handbrake. She depressed the clutch and found neutral. The trembling in her right hand made it difficult to turn the key in the ignition.

Her gaze followed the running youths. The group was gaining ground. The lone sprinter was tiring. He was gasping and spluttering, striving frantically to reach McDonalds on the corner. The harsh pool of light that flooded the forecourt encircled him in a giant halo, turning his face a sickly green. He hesitated before jumping the low, wooden fence. Leading with his left leg he cleared the hurdle, but his right foot tapped the wood. He stumbled, staggered for a few strides, steadied himself and was upright again. Too late! His five tormentors were on him like a pack of hounds with fresh prey. They grabbed him and brought him down, squealing and shouting.

Aftermath

She had to do something. She couldn't just sit gawking and do nothing. She reached for her mobile phone but it wasn't in the side pocket where it should have been. She fumbled in her bag: not there either. She heard her daughters' irritated voices, 'For goodness sake, Mother, what's the point of having a mobile phone if you never take it with you?'

Without thinking, she was out of the car and running towards the main door of the restaurant. She'd get help there. Surely someone would help her.

She shuddered as she heard the grunts and groans coming from the huddle of bodies, made a wild lunge at the door and then she stopped. She'd heard something else. The unmistakable sound of helpless laughter — loud, unrestrained laughter filled the space behind her.

Anne turned slowly and saw the young men struggling to stand upright. They wobbled about like giant jellies, laughing, shouting and aiming playful blows at each other.

'You fat bastard, you couldn't win a race for geriatrics,' shouted one.

'You can talk! You were miles behind. You're like a pregnant whale with that belly.'

'Come on ya bastards! Last to the counter is a Villa supporter.'

Feeling drained and slightly foolish Anne returned to her car and headed for home.

*

She indicated left and turned into the crescent where she lived. As she came alongside a parked car the passenger got out, but the driver stayed put. Anne glanced in the rear-view mirror and saw a young man, dressed in dark sports-clothes, sauntering along the pavement to her right. Instinctively she flicked the lever of the central-locking system and then quickly reprimanded herself for her panicky reaction. She'd already made a fool of herself that evening. She needed to calm down and keep her imagination under control. Besides, the bloke was way behind her.

She turned left onto her drive, applied the handbrake, switched off the engine, then the lights and put the gear stick into reverse. Once again she glanced in the rear-view mirror and thought she saw a flicker of movement by the privet hedge. She looked quickly around but there was no one there. She remained in the locked car and checked again. There was definitely no one there.

She was getting jumpy: time for a stiff drink, a hot bath and bed.

*

Her house was squeezed between the twin beacons of light coming from either side. At number eight the lights blazed through the curtainless window. The living-room vibrated with the warmth of family activity. Everyone was home at number twelve — light seeped through the blinds and both cars were parked on the drive. Outside in the misty darkness everything was quiet.

Aftermath

Anne liked when her neighbours were in: their presence made her feel safe and protected.

She was glad to be home. She stood at her front door, handbag tucked under her left arm. She placed the key in the lock and turned it. It didn't work so she jiggled it about. The lock clicked and the door groaned open against her weight. She put her left foot onto the concrete doorstep and it was then she heard the pounding footsteps on the path.

*

Her immediate instinct was to move quickly — to run — but she couldn't. Her limbs were melting like wax near a hot flame. Pulled irresistibly towards what she feared was behind her, she turned and saw the figure bearing down on her. There were two possible escape routes, but one was cut off. The other was the safety of her own home, but everything was happening too fast and her legs wouldn't move, were incapable of acting on the frantic message from her brain which screamed that she should get inside and slam the door.

She stood transfixed, as though caught in the glare of blinding headlights.

*

He was tall, muscular and moved with ease. His face was shrouded in the depths of a hood. The light from number eight didn't quite reach him. His hand shot out and grabbed for her bag. She felt the strong tug but she held on.

'Don't do that,' she said, as though talking to a naughty child. At the sound of her feeble remonstrance an hysterical giggle welled in her throat. She tried again. 'I said don't do that,' she repeated, her voice rising in anger. He said nothing but pulled harder and she could feel the power of his youthful strength. 'Don't do that,' she said again, but this time her voice was feeble and quiet and her legs started to buckle.

A fist caught her a glancing blow on the side of the head and she fell to the ground, landing on her knees. With one last tug he claimed the bag, turned and ran.

She heard the slam of a car door and at last opened her mouth and screamed.

*

Figures streamed from the neighbouring houses. Sakeena from number eight wrapped her in a motherly hug and urged her two eldest sons to jump into their car. They drove off, tyres squealing, in a futile attempt to catch the thief. Sajida from number twelve rang the police, the doctor and Anne's daughters and made cups of tea.

Later, as she lay in bed, calmed by the sounds of Sue and Clare moving quietly about the house, the breathy voice of the Radio Four presenter came back to her. She tried to remember what had been said. Something about 'brief moments': something to do with 'aftermaths'.

Aftermath

But she couldn't focus: the pills the doctor had given her were dragging her into a deep sleep. Tomorrow, she thought, I'll think about it tomorrow.

*

She woke the next morning, drowsy and heavy with sleep, her mouth thick and parched. Within seconds a wave of unfocussed panic engulfed her, and then she remembered. She closed her eyes and saw a young man, powerfully built, his face shrouded in a hood, loom out of the darkness. As his hand shot towards her she opened her eyes and shouted for her daughters.

She lay sweating and trembling, waiting for them to come.

*

Although they took some persuading, she shooed Clare and Sue out the door to work. 'I'll be fine,' she said, not at all sure that she would. As she sat by the comforting glow of the fire, wrapped in her dressing-gown, she remembered the events of the previous evening and shivered with fright. She could hear the pounding of feet, feel the blow that had knocked her to the ground and had left a blue-black bruise on her temple.

She started nervously at a knock on the door. For a moment she considered ignoring it, but then she went to the window, pulled back the net curtains and peeped through the tiny slit. She sighed with relief when she saw her neighbour's familiar figure.

As she had done the previous night, Sakeena wrapped her in a comforting embrace and Anne allowed herself to rest against the amble bosom, breathing in its milky, maternal smell.

Sakeena bustled about, setting a tray for tea, cutting the cake she'd brought into fat slices. 'Your daughters must come home and live with you,' Sakeena insisted. 'It's not right for a woman to live by herself, and you have plenty of room for them.'

Anne answered her with a faint smile.

*

She showered and dressed, then returned to the kitchen to prepare the evening meal. She put a bottle of wine to chill and made a special effort in setting the table, plucking up courage to venture into the garden for a few sprigs of winter-flowering Jasmine that grew close to the house.

She would enjoy the evening with her daughters; draw comfort from their presence. Tomorrow she'd send them on their way, back to their own lives. Then she'd start the process of reclaiming hers.

Somebody's Son

Tackler slung his alpaca jacket over his shoulder and swaggered towards the mirror. He struck a smouldering pose, allowed a ghost of a smile to flit across his face and raised his left eyebrow as though quizzing his own image. Pleased with the response he swung towards the door.

Brass monkeys: that's what Baz had said on the blower, so he had to wear something warm. His didn't want his Ma burning his ear-hole if he made his escape in his gear. And he had to escape. He was eighteen today. It was time.

*

'Turn it up, will you? I love this song. It's only gorgeous!'

'What? What did you say, woman?'

'I SAID, WILL YOU TURN IT UP?'

'YOU MUST BE FECKIN' DEAF, TO SAY NOTHING OF BEING DEMENTED IF YOU WANT TO LISTEN TO THAT EEJIT CATERWAULING. AS SOON AS WE'VE MOVED THIS SOFA I'M OFF FOR A PINT.'

'THERE'S NO NEED TO SHOUT, TOM BRADY, AND DON'T USE THE MUSIC AS AN EXCUSE FOR GOING TO THE PUB. DON'T YOU LIVE IN THAT

PLACE AND I DIDN'T EXPECT TODAY TO BE ANY DIFFERENT.'

*

The past month had been grot. Tackler had felt like a fish wriggling helplessly on the end of a tangled line. He knew he had to tell his Ma about his plans, but the glow of love in her eyes, the pleasure of her anticipation which he could almost smell, made him bottle out each time. He wished the family thing didn't mean so much to her, that she'd let him get on with what he wanted to do, that she'd just let go. It was like been loved by an octopus: tentacles tightening round him until he could hardly breathe. And there was no escape in sleep. In his dreams he spent his eighteenth birthday cavorting madly with his Aunt Maggie in a wild jig which changed to a reel, then to a hornpipe and back to a jig again until he became a river of sweat.

His mates couldn't see the problem. To them it was simple. 'I'm going up town for a few drinks with the lads, Ma. I'll be home on the last bus.' That's all he had to say. But they hadn't the whole bloody clan camping out all over the kip.

As he stepped onto the landing the house trembled to the rhythms of his Ma's favourite reel. The fiddle, bodhran and banjo combined in a riotous bowing, beating and plucking and built to a deafening crescendo. Shit! They'd hear him coming and he'd have to 'pass himself', which meant kissing his Ma, his Gran and Aunt Maggie. He was not going to kiss his Da or Uncle Bren, and the poxy neighbours could take a run and jump.

He checked the strides, brushed his hand through his long, dark hair and sauntered downstairs.

*

Breda let her end of the sofa drop and hurried past Tom to the kitchen. He could shift the friggin' thing himself. A mixture of emotions jangled through her strong, sinewy body. A sense of pleasure, of something achieved, battled with a feeling of rejection.

Back in the strange environs of Derry she'd always felt nervous about the safety of her sons. Unease stalked her at a distance and then, as Eamon started secondary school and the civil rights movement grew, it pounced, gripped her heart in a vice of fear and refused to let go. The battle of the Bogside had frightened her so much she'd had a seizure. For years she hadn't dared think of her sons growing to maturity. Each birthday, as Eamon notched up another year, she ticked off the secret calendar she'd locked inside her. Where they had lived many boys didn't get to grow up: few of them had little to celebrate if they did. But since they'd moved to Birmingham, she'd allowed herself to dream and she'd woven her dreams into a warm blanket of love and hope. So it was time to celebrate.

She'd decided she'd invite all the family — grandparents, aunts, uncles and cousins. They would hire a hall to fit them all in. They might even have the Kilfenora Ceilidh Band — the best in the whole of

Ireland — and they would get private caterers to do the food. She'd let Tom organize the drink; he'd be good at that.

Of course she'd had to modify her dreams, but she refused to relinquish them altogether. She was certain that on this night, if god spared them, they would spend the evening together celebrating the coming of age of her first-born. And he had spared them, and Eamon was going up town with his friends and Tom was going to the pub for a pint.

*

'I'm off now, Ma.'

'Are you sure you have to go? Can you not stay here and ask your friends to come over?'

'Leave the lad alone, Breda. He's a man now. It's only right and proper that he goes out with the lads for a few pints.'

'Isn't he going to do that on Saturday with a whole crowd from college? It wouldn't hurt him to stay in tonight.'

'Ma, Da, I've gotta go. The lads just want to go up New Street and buy me a drink for my birthday. I'll be back early like I said.'

'Remember, Eamon, no later than nine. Your grandma likes to be in bed by ten and she wants to see you blow out the candles.'

*

She had to stop mollycoddling the lad. It was comin' the heavy to expect a young man to do cartwheels at the prospect of spending an evening jigging and reeling with a crowd of ould ones. The thought of it made Tom feel queasy let alone a strapping lad like Eamon who had lots of young ones making eyes at him. But sure wasn't he a chip off the old block?

When Tom had been a wee lad in Derry he'd had his fair share of mots. Young women with pale skin and grey-green eyes and an abundance of rich, black hair that blew wildly as they walked by Lough Foyle. He no longer remembered their names. Over the years the melody of their soft voices and the music of their excited laughter had melded together and what came to him when he turned his thoughts to those times was a feeling of warmth, a feeling of gratitude.

*

'KUNG FU FIGHTING. UGH! UGH!' Tackler, Baz, Dave and Paul yelled at the top of their voices as they strutted towards New Street. Up on her plinth, like a Christmas pudding with a crown, Victoria scowled at Dave as he stopped suddenly and with knee bent, lifted his right leg to his waist and aimed for Paul's groin. Paul had seen it coming, executed a dazzling pirouette, reached out his hand, caught Dave's heel and brought him to the ground.

'Don't mess with the big boys, titch,'

'Big shit, you mean.'

'Right, where are you guys going to buy my first legal drink?'

'What about Yates'?'

'That's too far. I'm dyin' of thirst.'

'Let's start at the Windsor. The night is but a pup.'

'KUNG FU FIGHTING. KUNG FU FIGHTING. UGH! UGH!'

Tackler hadn't told his mates about his curfew. Their great guffaws of laughter played like a kettledrum in his head as he imagined announcing, 'Our Mum says I've got to be home by nine o'clock so my Gran can see me blow out my candles.'

The lads went to college together and played for the football team. It was Dave who'd given him his nick-name. He no longer answered to Eamon, except at home. Tackler was who he was: was what he did. He'd take the ball and run like the wind, weaving and dodging, selling dummies and then running again. But what he enjoyed most was thieving the ball from another player. No rough stuff: just skill.

'Go for the ball, not for the man,' that's what his Da had told him when he first started playing soccer on the windswept fields of Derry. 'Sure any eejit can hack another player. It takes a good footballer to steal the ball before his opponent cops on.'

Bobbie Moore was his hero. To see Moore was to see music — harmony, rhythm, tempo. He'd watched Moore play at Villa Park. After The World Cup he'd pestered and pestered his Da until he'd caved in and he'd taken them to stay with friends in Birmingham. His Da, his younger brother and himself had stood squashed in the Trinity Road End amongst thousands of fans, lashed by the winter rain and buffeted by the wind.

Somebody's Son

He was ten, and his young heart had almost burst with joy and pain as Moore performed his magic right there in front of his eyes.

*

'He's not going to be the ghost at the feast, is he?'

'What are you talking about?'

'Well, you've gone to all this bother and he's not even here.'

'He'll be back by nine. Now stop your blatherin' Maggie Maguire and help me make these sandwiches.'

'Does Eamon still play football, Breda?'

'Of course he does, but he's more interested in his studies these days, so he only plays on Sundays.'

'Ah, it's a shame he didn't make the grade.'

Breda took a plate from the cupboard and let the door shut with a bang. She slammed a pile of sandwiches onto the plate and, with a deft flick of her strong wrist, tore a sheet of greased paper from its roll and wrapped it tightly round the food.

'What are you talking about?'

'Sure didn't he always want to be a professional footballer?'

'He did not. He loves doing his 'A' levels. He's a born academic, that's what they've said at the college. When he's finished there, he's going to do English and Philosophy at university.'

'Study can be very stressful. Many's the one has a complete mental breakdown from the pressure of it. I think it's best avoided if you're not really suited to it.'

'Will you pass me the mayonnaise?'

*

Nothing changes and everything changes. Growing up in Dublin Maggie had been the sister who attracted attention and had been indulged. Breda had learned early that her dark hair and pale-grey eyes could not compete with Maggie's abundant blond ringlets and her blue eyes which were the colour of the sea on a warm summer's day. Maggie's beauty blossomed as she matured and at the peak of her perfection she was claimed by Brendan Maguire, a young student from County Derry.

Breda had met Tom at Maggie's wedding. Tom, the carpenter from the Bogside, was an unlikely friend for the rich, landed Brendan, but it was their love of football that brought them together. Resisting the pressure to play Gaelic, Tom had opted for soccer. Resisting the pressure to play rugger, Brendan had made the same choice. And they were good: they played for the county. And they were good friends and Breda would always be grateful to Brendan because it was his friendship that had saved Tom.

*

The warm, smoky atmosphere of the Windsor wrapped them in a comforting fug. Baz had been right, it was brass monkeys outside and he was glad that they'd made this pub their first watering-hole. The upstairs room was long and narrow with walls the colour of sick but it was warm and snug and it

Somebody's Son

reminded Tackler of the homely bars in Derry where his Da used to drink.

He sipped the pint of Guinness his mates had bought him. Usually, when he could get served in a pub, he drank bitter, but tonight for his first legal drink, he'd chosen stout.

Throughout his childhood, at every family occasion — celebration or wake — he'd observed his Da's ritual as he prepared to drink a glass of creamy porter. First his Da would search in his pocket for the brass bottle-opener he always carried with him. 'A man's not properly dressed without his wee opener,' he'd say. He'd unfold his large, white hanky and wipe the opener until it gleamed. Then he'd take the bottle in his big, rough hands and gently prise the top off. The next step was the most important. His Da would hold the glass at a slight angle and pour the dark-brown liquid, slowly and carefully, taking his time, never rushing, until eventually he would hold the glass aloft, assessing the balance of the liquid and thick creamy top. He would take his first sip, sigh with deep satisfaction and lick the residue of foam from his top lip.

Sometimes he'd let Tackler and his cousin Vin have a sip and they would strut about, little men cut short, with foam moustaches. Vin and himself were the same age and they'd done everything together: hiked in the Scalp Mountain, played football, thrown stones at the Brits. Sometimes now, as he played football, he thought he could hear Vin urging him to get 'the lead out and get the feckin ball'. Sometimes he thought he saw him running like a hare as he'd done countless times through the back streets of Derry. But he wouldn't be seeing Vin again. The battle of the Bogside had drawn him to the barricades where he'd been hit by a bullet. His young blood had left a crimson stain on the street that took weeks to fade.

*

'You're a noisy lot.'

Tackler turned at the sound of the voice. The girl he'd spotted when they'd first come in was standing next to him at the bar. She was slim; tall for a girl, with long, dark hair. Her face was small and oval and she had intelligent eyes which, as she met his gaze, seemed to hold something in reserve. He liked the way her face softened when she smiled, he liked the glint of her ear-rings as she brushed her hair back from her face and he liked the freckles sprinkled across her cheeks.

'I haven't made a sound for the past ten minutes.'

'Your mates are making enough noise for twenty.'

'Sorry about that, we're celebrating. Can I get you a drink?'

'No, ta. When I finish this we're off.'

'Stay for another. It's early.'

'We're meeting some mates across the road. We said we'd be there by eight and we're late already.'

'Tell you what, I'll get the lads to drink up and we'll come and join you, how's that?'

'Yeah, great, bostin'. See you soon. Tarar, a bit.'

Somebody's Son

'Hey, I don't know your name or where you're going.'

'It's Diane, and we're going to the Tavern in the Town.'

*

Everything changes and nothing changes. Tom ducked deeper into the collar of his donkey jacket. He felt the raw air slice at his face, but he was glad to be out of the house. It was his son's eighteenth birthday, but he wasn't really in the mood for celebrating. He was making his way to the nearest pub, but he didn't really want to go there.

There was little to comfort him wherever he turned. He felt that fate was following him like a hungry hound and there was no chance of escape. He didn't dare share his fears with Breda: couldn't bear the thought of her pale-grey eyes empty of love and filled with accusation.

It was her eyes that had enticed him when they'd first met, although his first glimpse of her had not been promising. She'd stood, awkward and gaunt, in her pink bridesmaid's dress, like a giant stick of Blackpool rock. Her dark hair refused to be tamed by the piece of frippery attached to it and escaped here and there in unbecoming tufts. As one of Brendan's groom's men he'd felt obliged to invite her to dance. A man of graceful movement and natural rhythm, he had no great expectations of the young women who held herself in such a stiff, unyielding manner. But as 'My Blue Heaven' boomed around the red and gold splendour of the Shelbourne Hotel ballroom, Tom took Breda in his arms and was pleasantly surprised. She responded to the rhythm and tempo and her body softened and relaxed. She moved easily across the floor, mirrored his steps and matched his energy.

When the dance was over, they stood laughing and breathless. She looked at him with her pale-grey eyes and he could see the depth and the longing in them.

He'd taken her from her beloved Dublin to the northern town of Derry where she'd been unnerved by the fierce tribal loyalties. The menace and threat which he took for granted as the Apprentice Boys marched and lit their fires every August, sent her scurrying to a darkened room. If she couldn't hear the clamour, couldn't see the flaming daubs of orange against the summer sky, she could feel herself and her family safe.

He'd inherited a long tradition of republicanism. His grandfather had been active in earlier struggles and his father, who believed fervently in a united Ireland, had operated on the fringes.

Like all teenagers it had been Tom's instinct to challenge: he wanted no truck with the past. But he learnt that political conviction doesn't necessarily grow out of family tradition. It's born and nurtured as a result of personal experience and the discrimination and harassment that he'd endured in his native city made a reluctant rebel of him.

But he hadn't the courage to stay and see it through. And he was forced to ask Brendan for help, to flee to Birmingham with Breda and the boys, to stay

Somebody's Son

a nightmarish six weeks with friends before they found their own place.

*

Everything was ready. The salty, fatty smell of pigs' trotters set the juices flowing as it mingled with the earthy smell of porter. The music was leppin' and everyone was having a good time. To make the evening complete she needed her husband and her eldest son. She wished they'd come home, wished they'd come in out of the cold, damp night and enjoy the warmth and glow of a house filled with laughter and merriment.

She knew she clung too fiercely to Eamon. She knew he yearned for independence and freedom: that he didn't want to hurt her, but that he needed to leave her behind and strike out on his own. But she wasn't ready yet. Not yet. It was too soon. So she clung to him like a limpet to a rock, resisting the waves of his struggle.

Tom was struggling too and he wouldn't talk to her about what was troubling him because she'd made it impossible for him to do so, didn't really want him to.

She'd been glad to leave Derry. From the beginning the place had stifled her spirit and made her afraid, but she endured it because, when she married Tom, for the first time in her life she'd been the centre of someone's world. Tom loved her and in gratitude she loved him back with all the power and strength of her hungry heart and her strong, young body.

She knew nothing of his activities until he came home, one afternoon, breathless and agitated, having been tipped off that the house would be raided that night. He told her nothing else, but he took a parcel from behind their wardrobe, left the house and drove to Maggie and Brenden's. And that's all she knew.

Breda begged to return to Dublin, but Tom refused. It was too close and it was too dangerous. They had to get out of the country. Birmingham seemed a good choice. They had friends there and Tom could get work.

So that's what they'd done and the boys had settled in and blossomed, glad to be away from the daily grind of harassment and fear. And she was glad too. She was weary of hearing of young men maimed, killed and imprisoned. She couldn't find it in her heart to rejoice when the enemy was shot. All of these youngsters were somebody's sons. Somewhere a mother grieved for each one of them. And she didn't want to have to grieve for her sons.

She'd put Dublin on the back-burner. Some day she'd return to its elegance, to its long, golden strands, and its soft, ancient hills. Until that time she was content to see her family safe and well.

*

The pub had been worse than Tom had feared. Everyone was on edge. The talk was about the McDade funeral and the shenanigans at the airport. People were beginning to feel the heat. What with all the bomb scares in the city the Irish were not wanted and there was a feeling that there might be a backlash.

Most of the men just wanted to keep their heads down. They didn't want any trouble. Many had children who'd been born in the city and felt they had a stake in England and, consequently, they suffered the pull and drag of divided loyalties. There were some who were pleased that the fight was being brought to the enemy, but they were mostly young, unmarried, without children of their own.

He hadn't discussed the worsening situation with Breda. He knew she was blocking it out, focussing all her fierce love on her family and getting on with daily life. Besides, he was reluctant to re-open arguments that circled without end. He was sad and angry too, that she couldn't see that his love for their sons was as warm as her own; that his greatest joy was to see them growing into healthy, young men who enjoyed their football, did well at their studies and fitted in.

He didn't want Breda and himself to drift apart like two ships that had slipped their moorings. He wanted them to rediscover the intimacy of their earlier years when they crossed the border into Donegal, walked for miles on Bundoran strand and made wild plans. They'd save hard and return to Dublin and buy a house in Killiney, overlooking the sea. Or maybe they'd buy land outside Derry and breed horses. Or maybe they'd just travel the world: the two of them together, away from all the trouble and strife of their homeland.

Tom quickened his step: he wanted, desperately, to be home with his family.

As he rounded the corner into his road a burley figure came out of the dark and almost sent him sprawling.

'Watch what you doin', O'Farrell.'

'Tom, I'm sorry Tom. Have you heard the news?'

'What news? What do you mean?'

'Oh, Jesus, Tom, it's desperate, it's feckin' desperate.'

*

The room shook with the sound of jollity. The fiddle, banjo, bodhran and accordion picked up the tune in turn, melded together, and then soared away on their lone riffs once again. Feet slapped and stomped the floor as the dancers swirled in abandonment, twirling faster and faster until the music reached a resounding crescendo.

Breda collapsed onto the nearest chair, sweating and laughing. It was well past nine and Tom and Eamon hadn't come home, so she'd decided to go with the flow, to enjoy herself. She was not going to waste her hard work and effort.

The music started up again and Brendan pulled her to him and they were waltzing to the strains of 'My Lagan Love' when Breda heard the front door bang. At last! One of them was back, or maybe they'd both come together. She abandoned Brendan and ran towards the hall.

'Is he home?'

Somebody's Son

'No, sure he's as bad as yourself, Tom Brady.'
'Is he not home?'

Slowly, Breda realized that there was something wrong. Tom's usual ruddy complexion was ashen, ghostly. His deep-set eyes were bulging and he seemed unable to blink.

'Something terrible's happened, Breda. Something terrible.' She didn't answer. She stilled herself, became rigid.

'There's been an explosion, two explosions, in New Street...'

'Oh Jesus...'

'Two bombs...'

'Oh Jesus, no. Not my son.'

'In two pubs in the city ...'

'Oh, no, Jesus, no, not my son. Please, god, not my son.'

Breda's desperate plea was followed by a haunting banshee wail. Her strong frame lost its rigidity and bent double, and she screamed again, drowning out the strains of 'My Lagan Love' which played on and on in the background.

'DEAR GOD! DON'T TAKE MY SON.'

Tom moved towards her and suddenly she sprang at him. Like a cat mad with fear she attacked him, clawed at him, howling her anguish. He caught her arms and, exerting all his strength, pinned them to her sides. She struggled and fought as family and friends looked on, numbed and paralysed. She screamed again and again.

At last the music stopped and Breda's entreaty filled the silence.

'I WANT MY SON. I WANT MY SON...'

Tom focussed all his attention on his wife. She needed him now, this minute. But soon, when she'd quietened, he would go into the city and look for their son.

PART III

Interlude

She woke with a jolt and glanced out the window. The plane was surrounded by water, within feet of its undulating surface. For a horrifying moment she thought they would plunge into the sea. Panic-stricken, she gripped the arms of the seat as they hurtled towards the heaving waves, but with a violent judder and jubilant roar they touched down on the rain-soaked runway.

*

She was not heartened by her first impression of Nice. As she waited for the bus to take her into the city centre the sky was dark and leaden with unspent rain and a cruel wind whirled round her legs. She was bitterly disappointed. She remembered her teenage self, collapsing in hysterical giggles as Pauline declared, *'Oui, Mon Amie,* we are off to the Frrrrench Riverrra to soak up the sun and to sojorrrrn with Claude and Pierre on their huuuge yacht.' Of course their silly plans had come to nothing, but now that she'd finally made it, she found the glamour of her adolescent daydreaming had been an illusion: the South of France was as grey and dull as the England she'd abandoned a couple of hours previously.

Interlude

She made her way through streets festooned with posters of a hawk-faced man who looked familiar, but whom she couldn't quite place.

After what seemed an age she finally arrived at her hotel. Her room was small, with smoke-stained walls, heavy striped curtains and a bedspread of cream and blue dots on an ochre background. Two single beds were pushed together to make a double and a scratched table and two worn chairs stood close to the French window that opened onto a narrow balcony. There was little evidence of 'the tasteful refurbishment' mentioned by the travel agent, but she welcomed the drabness of the room: in her present mood anything cheerful would be unbearable.

Exhausted, she lay on the bed, and fell immediately into a deep sleep.

*

Three hours later Bridget woke, sweating and confused. She was surrounded by strange sounds and smells: the quiet of her suburban garden replaced by the roar of cars accelerating and the angry buzz of speeding motorcycles; its fragrance by a pungent mixture she couldn't identify.

She struggled from the bed, stumbled to the window and stepped onto the balcony. The Holiday Inn sign, emblazoned on the ugly concrete building opposite, gave no clue as to her whereabouts. She leaned out over the railing, glancing to her left. An elegant apartment building gleamed in the twilight, its façade festooned with delicately-worked iron balconies. She remembered where she was, and the impulsive act that had brought her there: remembered how the need to escape had gripped her like a metal straightjacket; had squeezed her until she thought she would snap.

On her way home from town she'd called into Co-op Travel on the High Street, not sure what she intended. After a ten-minute wait she found herself telling the young assistant that she wanted to visit a European city, wanted to leave the next day. It was Easter week-end so all flights to Rome were completely booked, Prague likewise, also Paris and Barcelona, the young woman told her, her lips tight with annoyance. However, she could get her on a flight from Birmingham to Nice.

At the mention of the name Bridget had a flashback to her teenage self and without hesitation booked a seat.

Less than twenty-four hours later she'd arrived at her destination.

*

A missed period had caused her to bolt: run away like a startled horse, unable to wait for Matt's return in case she might blurt out the news. She heard her mother's voice. 'You've a reckless streak that will be the ruination of you one of these days, my girl,' she'd enjoyed telling Bridget, over and over again. For the first time in her life Bridget was willing to concede that her mother might be right about something.

Interlude

She glanced at her watch and read eight o'clock. If that was local time, if she'd adjusted her watch on the plane, it was seven o'clock in England and Matt would be arriving home from the residential in Malvern. 'No doubt another round of strategies to teach us how to cope with the collapse of the National Health,' he'd said, with a mirthless laugh, as he'd kissed her goodbye two days previously. He would open the front door, drop his keys on the hall table and call her name. She allowed herself to visualize him as he moved from room to room and then into the garden, trying to find her. She saw the shrug of his slim shoulders and the look of puzzlement on his handsome face when he failed.

She wondered how long it would be before he checked his emails.

*

Half an hour later she was walking along the Promenade des Anglais feeling both excited and nervous. The sea pounded the beach to her right with only the frothy foam visible in the dark. Strung out along the front opposite elegant hotels and restaurants threw beacons of light across the pavement and offered an endless supply of delicious foods and wines. The Promenade was busy. A mixed gaggle of Europeans, Americans and Japanese had come to join the perambulating locals in taking the evening air.

Although ravenously hungry she put off choosing a restaurant. Protected by the presence of Matt or of her many friends she never dined out alone and always felt sympathy, bordering on pity, for women who did. Observing them as they ate, eyes averted or riveted to a book, she'd hoped fervently that she would never have to do the same, but the thought of waiting until morning for the continental breakfast offered by her hotel focussed her mind. She'd have to pluck up courage and find a place to eat.

Four lanes of fast-moving, hectoring traffic divided the polarities of the pounding sea and the Belle Époque buildings. Bridget moved towards a crossing and waited for the lights to change. She felt the presence of someone standing too close and, without thinking, stepped into the oncoming traffic. A hand shot out and grabbed her arm. 'You must be careful, Madame,' a deep voice said in heavily accented English, 'the French are reckless drivers.' Bridget pulled her arm from the firm grip and, as the lights changed, hurried across the road and into the first restaurant she came to.

*

A tall waiter, his figure draped in an olive-green apron, greeted her. *'Bonsoir, Madame,'* he said. *'Vous rejoignez quelqu'un ce soir?'* At her look of incomprehension he translated for her. 'Are you joining someone this evening, Madame?'

'No,' she said and then, determined to use her rudimentary French added, *'Une table pour une personne, s'il vous plait.'* With a smile and a slight bow he led her to a table next to a large umbrella plant, handed her a menu and left.

Her heart sank when she glanced at the list of dishes: there was no English translation and she knew her French wasn't up to it. She was about to make a hasty exit when the waiter reappeared. Before he could say a word she blurted out, *'Une bouteille d'eau minérale et un plat de jour, s'il vous plait.'* He opened his mouth to ask a question, saw the panic in her eyes and changed his mind. Instead he reached for the menu. Like a child clinging to a favourite toy she refused to let go.

Bridget allowed herself a swift glance round the room. At the other tables couples conversed in a leisurely manner or small groups laughed and chatted. She was the only person dining alone. She returned her gaze to the menu and cursed herself for forgetting to bring a book.

She jumped nervously as someone took a seat at the table the other side of the umbrella plant. A breeze from an open window stirred the leaves, they parted and she saw another lone diner. It was the stranger from the traffic lights.

*

Next morning she was drawn again to the Promenade des Anglais. She had given herself a goal: she would walk as far as Nice Port and find somewhere to lunch.

The weather had changed: the sea and the sky shone a brilliant blue and the city glowed with a feeling of well-being. Even at this early hour the

Promenade was bustling with activity. Like her, many simply strolled along, enjoying the morning sunshine and gazing at the azure sea that beat a thunderous rhythm on the pebbles below. Others walked with purpose, locals, she supposed, hurrying about their daily tasks. Cyclists, skaters and joggers sped by, twisting and weaving between pedestrians and each other, their movements choreographed by an invisible dance-master.

The Promenade was dotted with white, mettle seats facing outwards towards the sea or in towards the town. She sat down, choosing to gaze at the foaming surf. As she closed her eyes and raised her face to the sun she thought how good it was to be alive. The thought startled her. Only yesterday, in a fit of blind panic, she'd run away from home, from everyone she knew — from Matt. Today, after a restless night dreaming that she and Matt were chasing each other in ever-widening circles through narrow cobbled streets, she felt calm and at ease. Viewed in the light of her changed mood, her actions of the previous day seemed hysterical and foolhardy.

*

She continued her walk to the Port. To her left a statue of Athene rose, heroic and triumphant, against a backdrop of giant palms. A small train, offering trips to Le Château perched high on the hill overlooking the city, blocked her way so she moved from the sea wall to the outer-edge of the Promenade. The sight of oversized passengers, chins touching knees as they

Interlude

hunched in tiny carriages, brought to mind Gulliver in Lilliput and by association her native Dublin and she felt a surge of homesickness.

Averting her eyes she spotted the stranger who'd accosted her at the traffic lights the night before and had unnerved her by appearing in the restaurant. He was about twenty metres away and was hurrying in her direction. To the astonishment of an elderly couple she jumped into their cramped carriage and, in her haste, shut the gate with a resounding bang.

'*Pardon, Madame, Monsieur,*' she stuttered, in an attempt to assuage their alarm. Peeking round the handbag she was using to shield her face, she saw the stranger's receding back. Relieved, she stood up, cast an apologetic smile at the bemused couple and was about to disembark when the train jolted forward. She tried to steady herself, but everything was out of scale so she couldn't find a grip. The train gave another more violent jolt that sent Bridget onto the frail lap of her fellow passenger who let out a quiet moan. His wife's thin mouth opened a fraction and she emitted a mouse-like squeak of horror. As Bridget attempted to disentangle herself she wondered why the driver was delivering her commentary in such furious tones. Icily, Madame Mouse translated for her.

'You are putting us all in jeopardy by your thoughtless behaviour.' she said. 'The driver would like you to sit down and to stay in your seat until the train comes to rest at Le Château.'

*

Despite the rather ignominious start to the journey and the embarrassment she couldn't quite shake off as the train trundled round the narrow streets of the old town before climbing the hill to Le Château, she enjoyed the outing. Madame Mouse's disdain didn't perturb her unduly. She was used to this reaction from wives and girlfriends. They didn't, on first acquaintance, warm to her. Men, on the other hand, usually did. So when his wife was distracted by the charm of the old buildings or when she admired the spectacular panorama of Nice and the sea, revealed through the trees as they climbed higher and higher, Monsieur Mouse cast surreptitious glances at Bridget, and even dared the occasional flirtatious wink.

As they disembarked Bridget felt his hand brush against her thigh. She glared at him in rebuke and received another wink in reply.

*

She decided not to join the train for the return journey. At the top of the hill she stood drinking in the magnificence of the city. Below her, like a vast bouquet of multi-coloured flowers, lay a dense cluster of buildings, cream, blue, yellow and ochre. The azure-blue crescent of the bay framed the city to the east and snow-capped mountains rose, cool and resplendent, to the south.

Her thoughts were tugged back to another place and the Baie des Anges was overlain by a different image. She saw the sweep of Killiney Bay, about ten miles outside Dublin, its beauty more subdued, but no less enchanting. Matt and she had spent their honeymoon there. They'd rented a house that clung to the shallow cliff, its bay window jutting out over the sea, making them part of its shifting, watery world. Matt's gentle lovemaking had fired in Bridget a passion which surprised and delighted them both.

Each morning, after a leisurely breakfast, they strolled along the beach and then later in the day walked to Sandycove where Joyce's Martello Tower stood undeterred against the salty elements: or they would walk, instead, to Dalkey. As the fishermen steered their boats into the tiny harbour, they waited excitedly, like children awaiting a treat, to see what fish they'd eat that evening — sea bass, mackerel or plaice.

At the memory her eyes filled with tears and, with an involuntary movement, her right hand found the soft mound of her belly and stroked it gently.

*

A sly wind played underneath the warmth of the sun and its chill forced her to move. She started a slow descent through the Parc de la Colline du Château, allowing herself to be distracted by its many features: the exotic planting, the colourful mosaics of the bird and fish fountains, the artificial waterfall that fell in a sheer, silver sheet over a stony outcrop. She decided to give the inter-denominational cemetery where Catholics, Jews and Protestants were buried alongside each other a miss, and headed instead for the Flower Market in the Cours Saleya.

By the time she arrived most of the flowers had been sold, but the rich aroma of coffee and pastry tempted her, so she took a seat outside a café and watched as tourists ambled slowly from stall to stall. She sipped her coffee and almost slavered with delight as she bit into buttery pastry, liberally laced with dark, bitter chocolate.

Idly, she picked up a leaflet from the table. Black lettering printed on yellow contained the message, 'Email Café, the only one in the Old Town, seven terminals, 8 rue St Vincent'. She stared at it blankly for a few moments, then folded it and put it in her bag.

*

Back in her hotel she closed the window to deaden the incessant rumble of traffic, drew the curtains to block out the warmth of the sun and collapsed onto the bed. Her early morning sang-froid had melted away. She felt desolate and lonely.

She longed to talk to Matt, but knew she would weaken and tell him about her late period. She didn't want to hear the joy in his voice when all she could offer in return was panic and uncertainty.

For the first time since she'd left home Bridget allowed herself to think about the email she'd sent Matt from Birmingham Airport. In her haste she'd left the house without leaving a note and only remembered her omission when she spotted the internet terminals in the departure lounge. She thought to text him, but found she'd forgotten her mobile phone.

Interlude

She'd sat looking at the screen, unsure what to say. In the end she'd simply written,
Matt, I've had to go away for a while. I didn't plan it, it's a spur of the moment thing. I know you'll worry but I don't want you to. I'll be okay. Bridget.

Rousing herself she went to the window and opened the curtains. She sat on one of the battered chairs, picked up the yellow piece of paper from the table, read it once again, folded it, and put it in her bag.

Twenty minutes later she was walking through the streets of the old town searching for 8 rue St. Vincent.

*

When she at last found the café she went immediately to the room that housed the internet terminals. To her relief the young assistant spoke fluent English and within minutes she was left to her own devices. Her fingers trembled as she logged on to Hotmail, typed her email address and password. Her inbox showed five messages — all from Matt. She went straight to the fifth.

(12.10a.m.) Bridget, where are you? Please, please, get in touch. I'm frantic with worry. I don't know whether I should contact your mother. If I don't hear from you by morning I'll phone the police.
I love you,
Please come home.
Matt.

She clicked on reply and wrote;

I'm all right. Don't worry. I'm all right. Do not contact my mother.

She clicked 'send' and the message had gone.

*

For dinner she chose a café tucked away in a narrow street in the market area. She sat in a corner within the plastic awning that protected the diners from the chill of the spring evening. She ordered pizza and a glass of red wine, then changed her mind and had water instead.

As she ate she wondered if Matt would be able to trace her through her email. She knew any payments made on her credit or debit cards would be traceable so she had to be careful not to use up her supply of euros. She wondered if, two days previously when she'd walked into the travel agents, she had subconsciously been protecting herself against discovery, been unwilling to use the computer she shared with Matt to book online. The thought of her possible duplicity filled her with unease. She thought again about the email she'd sent him that afternoon. Perhaps she should have written more: tried to explain why she'd left so suddenly: why she had to get away. But she knew she had to sort it out in her own mind before she could explain to Matt, before she could hope to make him understand.

*

At nine o'clock she stepped into the lift that took her to the fourth floor of her hotel. Apart from the constant

Interlude

rumble of the traffic all was quiet. Unlike her, she supposed, the other guests were out and about enjoying the delights offered by Nice.

When she entered her room she closed the window, drew the curtains and switched on the wall lamp that cast a feeble light onto the table. Taking a pad of paper from a drawer she sat down and started to write.

'Dear Matt,' she began, *'I'm sorry to have left so suddenly, I'm sorry to worry you, but I need time to come to terms with what's happening to me. I need time to think things through, to decide what's best for me to do.*

For a long time now I've wanted to tell you how the idea and actuality of having a baby terrifies me, but I knew you'd shush me, laugh at my fears, point out how medical advances ensure virtually pain-free birth, that thousands of women come through the experience unscathed every day, that you'd take care of me.

I know all this, Matt, but it doesn't seem to help. At the moment I'm just so frightened. It's not just the pain, Matt. There are other things that send me into a blind panic. I wonder if other women are unnerved by the invasion of their bodies, by having another human being, living inside them, feeding off them, for nine whole months; if they're repulsed by their bellies growing bigger and bigger, like a gigantic balloon; If they find the thought of suckling a baby distasteful. It seems that my body would no longer be mine — someone else would have prior claim to it.

Is it unnatural for me to feel this way? I feel it must be as I've never heard any woman say these things. And I wonder how other women cope with the tearing and agony of the birth itself.

I'm not sure I can do it, Matt. Not sure I have the courage. I'm not sure I want to.

Bridget hesitated, read what she'd written, tore the page from the pad, crumpled it and threw it onto the bed.

*

'The railway station is about six hundred metres from here, Madame,' the receptionist smiled. 'Take a left out of the hotel, a right at the traffic lights and continue straight on.'

Bridget had decided to visit Monaco, twenty minutes away by train. She thought strolling around the tiny principality, visiting the palace on the hill, gawping at the casino in Monte Carlo might relax her, help her to forget her worries for a while, put things into perspective.

As she waited in the slow-moving queue with other passengers who intended to travel within the hour, she once again noticed the image of the arrogant, hawk-faced man emblazoned on every magazine on a nearby rack. At last she remembered who he was. She looked in vain for a picture of his female rival in the presidential race — not much fraternity or equality in Nice she thought.

At last she completed her purchase. Ticket in hand, and intent on finding the correct platform, she failed to

Interlude

notice the man who walked a careful distance behind her.

*

She emerged from the crimson marble of Monaco station and stopped, unsure where to go. The harbour, filled to bursting with gleaming yachts, lay directly in front. Apartments, packed tightly together, clung desperately to hills that rose steeply on three sides. Despite being yards from the open sea she felt hemmed in, stifled and slightly faint.

Without making a conscious decision she turned right and then followed the signs for the Prince's Palace. As she climbed the steep hill a cooling breeze rippled in from the sea and refreshed her.

She wandered around the forecourt of the yellow palace, mingling with other tourists. In the Jardin Exotique she found a seat in the shade and ate the rolls she'd saved from breakfast. When she tired of gazing out to sea she followed a path leading to the cathedral and entered its cool interior. Without thinking she joined a queue making its way up a narrow aisle towards the main altar. She wondered at the interest shown in the tombs of what was, after all, a minor royal family, until she discovered that there was just one tomb that captivated the crowd.

She heard her mother's voice, filled with pride, as she exclaimed, 'Grace Kelly is a proper lady, that's what she is. A credit to Ireland and a fit wife for any prince or even king, I'd venture. And she's only gorgeous. It's a pity he's not a bit taller though, then she could wear high heels. Every woman should wear high heels: they're very flattering to the ankle.'

The fact that Grace Kelly was American didn't deter her mother or Ireland from claiming her as their own. Although Bridget was born sixteen years after the event she felt, through her mother's repeated tellings, that she'd personally witnessed Princess Grace's triumphant visit to Ireland in 1961 when she and her Prince stood, dewy-eyed, outside the two-roomed cottage of the Kelly ancestors on the shores of Leg of Mutton Lake in County Mayo. 'She had no airs and graces about her and was so obviously at home in these humble surroundings,' her mother assured Bridget, 'that the entire nation opened their hearts and their homes to her.'

Bridget wondered how many of the tourists alongside her were drawn there by this Irish connection and with the thought came a longing for home.

*

As soon as she could she left the queue, hurried from the cathedral and lost herself in a tangle of narrow streets. But there was no escaping Ireland in Monaco. As she stopped to get her bearings, the piercing gaze of an iconic face stared at her from a shop window. Above the image of Samuel Beckett the notice read, 'Vague Memories Ireland of Yesterday. An exhibition of portraits, landscapes, and interiors.' Below, the venue was given as, 'Princess Grace Irish Library, 9 rue Princesse Marie de Lorraine, Monaco Ville.'

Interlude

'You want?' The shopkeeper stood on the doorstep, smiling her encouragement.

'Yes ... *oui, s'il vous plait* ...' Bridget stuttered. 'Is it far to the library?'

'*Non, non, Madame*, she said, pointing vigorously towards the end of the street. '*A gauche, Madame, à gauche.*'

*

A bustling woman in her late thirties opened the door to Bridget. Her hair was blonde and stubborn; a mass of wiry curls refusing to be tamed.

'You have come to see the library or the exhibition?' she asked. Unsure as to why she was there Bridget kept her options open.

'Both, please.'

The blonde curls bounced and bobbed as the librarian led Bridget through a narrow hall into a high-ceilinged room where all available wall space was covered with glass-fronted bookcases.

'Because of her family connections Princess Grace was extremely interested in the history and literature of Ireland,' the librarian told Bridget and two other visitors, 'and when she died so tragically, the royal family kindly donated her entire collection so that this library could be opened in her memory.'

Guiltily, Bridget suppressed a giggle as she heard one of her fellow visitors whisper in an unmistakable Dublin accent, 'Sure that was very noble of them, or maybe they just wanted to have a bloody good clearout.'

The picture of Beckett which had been replicated on the poster and which had drawn her to the library, hung on the wall directly opposite the door of the adjoining room, his image flanked by those of James Joyce and Oscar Wilde. She was disappointed by what she saw. Although the portraits were skilfully painted they were, in essence, no different from the dozens of images of these giants of the literary world that she'd seen over the years. The artist had found nothing new to reveal about his subjects. If an artist has nothing to add, Bridget thought, he should save his paint.

The paintings of men sipping porter in a traditional pub and of a golden-haired, young girl, posed in her Irish dancing costume, she dismissed as pure nostalgia. She wondered how the artist had fooled himself into thinking that there was anything 'vague' about the 'memories' he'd attempted to evoke. As far as she was concerned he was pandering to the market for sentimental, Oirsh tosh. She turned in disgust to leave the room and spotted another picture.

Like a child to water she was drawn towards a landscape in which gentle shades of purple, pink, green and the palest yellow floated in a drenching mist — shapes forming and reforming in endless swirls and eddies. The fathomless depth of land and vapour suggested the mysteries and memories of an ancient people — nebulous, amorphous, infinite — and Bridget felt its primitive pull. Blindly, eyes filled with tears, she made her way from the building and out into the narrow streets of Monaco.

Interlude

Nothing blocked out the noise of the traffic from her room that evening: the closed window and the drawn curtains were helpless against its incessant roar.

She was glad to return to her temporary home. Despite Monaco's pleasing aesthetics and the proximity of the sparkling sea, she had tired quickly of the conspicuous affluence. The opulence, evident at every turn as she walked around the harbour towards the casino at Monte Carlo, wearied her.

And there was something else: she couldn't shake off the feeling that she was being followed.

*

On her return to Nice she had stopped at an internet café close to the station and checked her emails. As expected there was another desperate request from Matt for her to return home, or at least to answer her mobile phone. There were also three from friends, perhaps recruited by Matt in an effort to get her to break cover. Ignoring her friends she wrote to Matt.

I'm safe and well. Please, please don't worry. I'm trying to work things out. Please give me time. I need time, Matt, a little more time. I love you. Bridget.

She didn't venture out again that evening. She'd stopped at the small supermarket around the corner from the hotel and bought a quiche, its rich filling liberally dotted with spinach and creamy-white cheese. She chose two sweet-smelling tomatoes and was unable to resist the heady redolence of ripe strawberries.

Having satisfied her hunger she continued where she'd left off the previous night. She sat at the scratched table, took the pad of paper from the drawer and began to write.

'Dear Matt,' she wrote, *'I've been to Monaco today and everywhere I went I was reminded of home. I saw a landscape painting of Ireland which seemed to exert a strange power. I felt I was being absorbed by it, drawn into a mythical world; merging with all the people of Ireland from the beginning of time.*

You'll probably think I'm losing the plot, that I've been drinking too much vin rouge. I know I sound fanciful, but perhaps pregnancy makes women fanciful; perhaps they become more susceptible to all things metaphysical; perhaps its nature's way of allowing them to cope with the enormity of the physical changes taking place in their bodies.

Matt, I wrote last night of how frightened I am of being pregnant and of having a baby and that's true. But I guess I know I'm not the only woman to feel like this, that it's not unusual for women to be scared of pregnancy. Anyone with half a brain and a little imagination must be scared witless by the bloody reality of giving birth and yet millions of women seem to cruise through the nine months, confident and proud like ships in full sail. I know they can't all be a cross between Athene and Demeter: some of them must be mere mortals like me.

Perhaps I could cope if that was the whole story. But there's something else, Matt, something I haven't

Interlude

told you, something I've never told anyone — not a living soul.

*

Next morning she headed for the Promenade des Anglais, eager to recapture the feeling of well-being she'd experienced two days previously. Turning left out of the hotel she failed to notice the man who walked down the steps of The Holiday Inn opposite and followed her as she took another left off Boulevard Victor Hugo. The heady aroma of coffee, garlic and freshly baked bread wafting from shops and cafes made her feel slightly queasy so she quickened her step and hurried towards the front. She recoiled from the multiple images of Sarkozy that filled every window. She'd seen that zealous gleam in the eyes of home-grown politicians and knew it boded ill for all but a privileged few.

It was a glorious morning and the Côte d'Azur lived up to its name. The sea reflected the turquoise-blue of the sky: their combined brilliance cloaked the city in a shimmering veil.

She walked through the Jardin de Albert, crossed the road and strolled in the direction of the Port, determined to reach it this time. Halfway to her destination she stopped, sat on one of the mettle seats and looked out to sea.

After a few minutes she turned to survey the hustle and bustle of the Promenade. A female skater caught her eye. Although dressed in the casual garb of the very young and listening intently to an iPod, she was, Bridget thought, probably the same age as herself.

Her movements were graceful and assured as she sped past to the rhythm of the music only she could hear. Using the toe of her right skate as a brake she came to an abrupt halt. Reversing, she completed a full circle, leapt spinning into the air and with a fluid action landed on the pavement and raced away. Within seconds she returned and repeated the routine.

Although walkers and cyclists thronged round her, the woman was oblivious to their presence. She seemed to be surrounded by an invisible shield that forced others to change course while she kept relentlessly on, inhabiting a place where no one else existed.

Bridget dragged her gaze from the skater, raised herself from the seat, and continued on her way to the Port.

*

While she stood watching the Corsica ferry slip its mooring and glide away from the quay, once again, she had a feeling of being watched. For a heart-stopping moment she wondered if Matt had discovered her whereabouts, had come to Nice and was following her. She looked right and then left, but Matt's tall, slim figure was nowhere in sight. As casually as she could manage she turned round and surveyed the tourists standing in small groups behind her. He was not there either.

Interlude

She was spending too much time alone, she thought, it was making her jumpy. If she wasn't careful she'd end up like her grandmother who'd believed that her dead husband had followed her everywhere for the fifteen years she'd survived him, 'Except to the lavatory, of course. Your grandfather was always a proper gentleman,' she'd told a bemused Bridget.

For lunch she chose a portside café. As she made her way through the closely-packed tables the soft grey of a man's woollen jacket caught her eye. It stirred a memory: she felt she'd seen it before, but by the time she manoeuvred herself into a seat and looked again in the direction of the jacket it had gone. She ordered French onion-soup and crusty bread and washed them down with cool, sparkling water.

The stir and commotion of the quay engrossed her. She was enthralled by the continuous stream of yachts that sailed in and out of port like a troop of aquatic dancers jockeying for position. Once again she was reminded of her native city and of the times she'd enjoyed similar scenes in Dún Laoghaire and Howth.

And then she sat bolt upright. She had seen that jacket before. She felt sure she had. She'd glimpsed it against the backdrop of the harbour in Monaco as she stood unsure where to go. She'd also seen it on her first night in Nice.

*

Back in her hotel she lowered herself into a bath of hot, fragrant water, hoping it would relax her and dispel the fears that had gathered like threatening shadows when she realized that the stranger from the traffic lights had been following her since their first encounter.

She tried to dismiss her fears as groundless; to convince herself that it was sheer coincidence that the man appeared wherever she happened to be. But counting the number of sightings — five in less than three days — she accepted reluctantly that there might be a more sinister explanation. Had Matt sent someone to spy on her? Impossible! The stranger had appeared on her first evening in Nice and Matt couldn't have known where she was at that time. She thought of human trafficking: she'd read terrifying accounts of women disappearing, being beaten up and fed drugs until they acquiesced and worked the streets. But she was sure that that sort of thing happened only to vulnerable women who had no one to look out for them.

*

Early next morning she set out for the railway station. She was going to Cannes for the day. She would not be intimidated into staying indoors.

She kept her gaze riveted on the coastline as the train raced towards its destination, determined not to look for the stranger in the grey jacket. As far as she was concerned he was of no account: he didn't exist.

Forty minutes later Bridget walked briskly towards Boulevard Croisette, where renowned hotels, shops and restaurants beckoned but, as usual, she couldn't

Interlude

resist the lure of the sea so she allowed herself to be drawn to the beach.

The morning was cool and still, the horizon eclipsed by swirling mist. Rays of sunlight burst through grey clouds, burnishing the sea into a sheet of gleaming silver. The bay stretched out in front of her, a seamless, ghostly world: unknown and unknowable.

Shivering in the damp air Bridget drew her pashmina closely round her. 'A shadowy land has appeared, as they tell.' A line of poetry she'd learned at school came to her and, in her mind's eye, Bridget saw a young nun, tall and gangly, standing in front of a class of twenty-five ten year-old girls. The nun was pointing to words on a blackboard with a long, rounded stick. Bridget could hear the tap of wood on wood as Sister Cahill beat out the rhythm of the poem the class was reciting, but she couldn't hear the words. She tried to recall the name of the poem or other lines, but nothing would come. She thought perhaps Yeats had written it, but then dismissed the idea.

When she reached the end of the Boulevard she sat on a bench beneath a cherry tree laden with pink blossom. She thought about what she'd written the previous evening and the purpose of her nightly outpourings. She hoped if she could write it all down, if she could bring herself to commit to paper the details of the event that had shadowed her for so long, that she would at last have the words to tell Matt, to make him understand. But she was finding it a slow and painful process.

At this rate I'll never be able to go home to Matt. I'll end up like Hugh O'Neil, she thought, rather hysterically. Sister Cahill had taught them about The Earl of Tyrone who'd run away with other vanquished and humiliated Irish chieftains in the seventeenth century and had spent the rest of his life exiled in Europe, a penniless, embittered drunk. The Irish had imbued this ignominious defeat with an heroic gloss, referring to it ever after as 'The Flight of the Earls', giving credence to the notion that flight in itself is somehow glorious.

Perhaps that's why I always run away, Bridget thought, maybe it's historically determined, perhaps I'll never settle down, perhaps I'm destined to wander the earth in search of …

Her overwrought musings were interrupted as she glanced towards the man who sat down beside her. *'Bonjour, Madame,'* said the stranger from the traffic lights. 'May I join you?'

'Why are you following me?' Bridget strove to keep her voice steady.

'Pardon, Madame, if I have alarmed you, but I thought you needed protection.'

'How could you know what I need? You don't know me.' He hesitated before answering.

'Not personally, of course, Madame, but I feel I know you well, nonetheless.'

'Please, go away and leave me alone or … or … I'll call the police.' As she issued her threat she looked into his face. His eyes, large and brown and suffused with sadness, were ringed with deep laughter lines and dominated his thin, pale face. His mouth was soft and full. With a pang she realized that his light-brown hair, cut tightly to his head, reminded her of Matt.

He murmured a quiet, *'Pardon'* and rose to leave. He hadn't gone far before Bridget called out.

'Please, Monsieur, please wait,' she said, and followed him.

*

They strolled along the Boulevard in the direction of La Palais des Festivals. The mist was lifting and slowly the sea came to life, rippling and flowing in the sun.

'My name is Bridget,' she blurted out.

'I am Etienne,' he said, smiling.

'I would like something to drink and perhaps a croissant,' Bridget ventured.

'Of course.' She followed him down the steps and onto the decking of a café where yellow umbrellas swayed in the strengthening breeze.

They sipped their drinks in silence. Eventually Bridget looked at her companion and asked, 'Why have you been following me?'

He stirred his coffee for a few seconds without answering and then looked directly at her. 'You looked so sad, so lost. I was worried about you.'

'Why should you worry about a complete stranger?'

'You seemed familiar to me; you reminded me of someone I know. I just wanted to be sure you were all right.'

A child ran along the sand, chasing a beach ball that the wind had taken.

'Do you always look out for people you don't know?'

'No,' Etienne said, avoiding her gaze, 'but perhaps I should. Perhaps we all should.'

Bridget smiled in triumph, 'Hy-Brasail!' she exclaimed, 'it's Hy-Brasail.' At Etienne's puzzled look she explained. 'It's the name of a poem I learned at school about a far-away mythical island, an illusionary place which men spent their lives trying to find.'

'Perhaps that is what we all do,' Etienne said.

Bridget looked out towards the sea. The child had reached the ball. As he lunged towards it, the breeze caught it once again and sent it bouncing and skipping along the beach. Defeated, the toddler sat with a resounding wallop on the sand. For a long moment his astounded gaze followed the ball as it continued its carefree journey, then he opened his mouth wide and let out a howl of rage.

*

'I hope I did the right thing, Madame,' the receptionist greeted her with a worried frown.' Bridget waited. 'A gentleman telephoned to enquire if you were staying at the hotel and I told him you were and that you were out, that you would probably return by early evening.'

'Did he leave his name or a message?' Bridget tried to sound casual.

'No, Madame, he said he'd ring again.'

Interlude

Bridget turned and hurried from the hotel. She retraced her steps towards the station, entered an internet café and logged on.

Matt, if you ring again I shall move on. Bridget.

*

That evening Etienne took her to a small, crowded local restaurant. The tightly-packed tables were covered with red and white check cloths; the crimson walls hung with oils depicting luscious fruit and vegetables. A stocky woman emerged from behind the bar at the rear of the room. She was elderly and walked with a slight limp. Her dark eyes shone with aggression as she asked in English, 'You wanna eat now?'

'Oui, Madame, si c'est possible?' Etienne replied.

'C'est possible, c'est possible, Madame answered querulously, pointing to a table next the wall.

'The food must be very good,' Bridget remarked when they'd climbed round two diners whose table was jammed against theirs.

'*Non,*' said Etienne. 'N*on,* people come to see Madame; she is revered by the locals and, of course, they come also to see Bruno.'

'Who's Bruno?'

'Madame's dog.'

The noise of the restaurant clattered round them. The couple at the adjoining table spoke in loud, expansive tones, almost shouting to make themselves heard. Bridget had nothing to say to Etienne that she was willing to share with thirty other diners so she ate a tangy tomato salad, liberally sprinkled with basil and sweet onion, in silence. Their main meal, a rich bouf bourguignonne, arrived and as their neighbours rose to leave Etienne took a sip of wine, looked at Bridget over the rim of the class and asked, 'Why did you run away?'

'What do you mean?'

'Why did you run away from your husband?'

'What makes you think I did?'

'You are a beautiful, young woman, you wear a wedding ring, you are alone in Nice and I think if you were simply on holiday you would not look so sad, so desperate.

Bridget's eyes glinted with anger. 'You have no right to ask such questions,' she said.

'*Pardon, Bridget, pardon*, but you must talk to someone. You must not do anything … rash.'

*

Tears streamed down her face and into the water of the bath. Etienne, whom she'd known a few days, had read so easily what Matt, seemed unable to grasp.

She'd tried to explain, to make Matt understand the sense of loneliness and worthlessness, the paralysing fear that had haunted her for as long as she could remember; that sometimes the feeling was so overwhelming she almost drowned in it.

But she couldn't tell Matt why she felt that way, couldn't bring herself to do it. So helplessly he'd held her close and tried to laugh away her anguish. His love, he said, was strong enough to banish a

Interlude

thousand demons, but she knew this wasn't true: even as he spoke his blue eyes were shadowed by fear and apprehension.

She cupped her breasts in her wet hands, stroked her warm belly, softly, tenderly. She rose from the bath, wrapped herself in a towel and went and lay on the bed.

A few minutes later she dressed and left the hotel

*

The clouds of the early morning had returned, obscuring the moon and stars, so she relied on the white, cresting foam and the sound of the waves to guide her to the water's edge.

She stood for a long time looking into the darkness and thought of Etienne. 'You must not do anything rash,' he'd said. But he knew she was already guilty of that so he obviously thought her capable of something more extreme. She wondered if he was right. She wondered if she had the courage to walk into the black sea and allow it to engulf her, slowly and gently, until she closed her eyes and gave herself up to its chilly embrace, putting an end to all the turmoil and pain.

Snippets of the half-remembered poem had returned throughout the day and now, as she stood listening to the sea, the final couplet came back to her. 'Night fell on the deep, amidst tempest and spray, And he died on the waters, away, far away!'

She saw a light flash to her right and willed herself to look at it. It started low down, near the water and climbed, burning brighter and brighter in the centre of a plane's undercarriage, like the great eye of a Cyclops. The plane banked sharply and headed out to sea. Bridget wondered about its destination: perhaps it was going to Birmingham where Matt fretted and worried, or maybe it was headed for Dublin where her mother lay, sleeping peacefully, unaware of her daughter's distress.

Shivering with cold and fright the certainty grew that she didn't want to die far from home, without Matt and alone.

She turned from the water and, slipping and stumbling over the stony beach, made her way to the Promenade where, high above her, the leaves of giant palms rattled like bones in the dark.

*

After breakfast next morning she returned to her room, placed the 'do not disturb' sign on the door handle, sat at the table and began to write. She continued to write for over an hour. Some of the pages she crumbled and cast aside, others she flung onto the bed to be read again.

The phone rang and she sat for a moment, dazed, unsure what to do. It rang again and she moved to pick it up. 'Madame, there is a gentleman on the line for you, shall I put him through?' the receptionist's voice was bright with professional goodwill.

Bridget hesitated and then replied, '*Oui, s'il vous plait.*' She held her breath while she waited and was

Interlude

flooded with relief and disappointment when she heard Etienne's voice.

'*Bonjour, Bridget.*' He sounded cheerful. 'I have been waiting for you outside the hotel. Are you o.k.?'

'I'm fine,' she said.

'I have devised a plan for the day.'

'Yes.'

'I would like to take you to the village of Eze in the hills outside Nice.'

'I'll be down in five minutes.'

*

They took the bus from the central bus station. When it had escaped the narrow streets and heavy traffic of Nice it wound its way higher and higher along the coast road until they reached what remained of the medieval city.

The warmth of the sun was held in check by a cooling breeze so it was an ideal day for clambering up the steeps hills of Eze. Bridget was impatient to climb to the top of the village. 'Four hundred and twenty nine metres above sea level,' Etienne told her with pride, as though he were somehow responsible for this amazing fact.

Ignoring the appeal of the narrow streets with their artists' studios, shops, restaurants and cafes, they headed towards the Jardin Exotique and from there to the remains of the castle. Narrow paths coiled round borders of agaves, aloes, spurges and cacti. The delicate smell of jasmine was carried on the breeze. Other pleasures awaited visitors later in the year.

Branches of wild roses cascaded over wrought-iron structures and decaying walls; abundant bougainvillea promised a profusion of colour.

At last they stood in the ruins of the castle and looked out over, what Etienne insisted, was one of the most beautiful panoramas of the Riviera. Bridget allowed him his claim: the view was indeed spectacular. The magical blue of the Côte d'Azur stretched for miles and miles, the colour deepened by the contrast of the verdant hills that framed it.

They sat for a long while, mesmerized by the beauty of the landscape and oblivious to the other tourists who swarmed like bees through the Jardin Exotique. Satiated at last they decided it was time to eat.

The narrow streets played tricks on them and they walked in circles, curling back on themselves, passing and re-passing the same stone buildings, walking repeatedly through the same archways until at last they emerged onto a tiny square.

Tables and chairs were placed in single file against an ancient stone wall; food was served from a counter that seemed to have been hacked from the side of the hill.

Etienne ordered crepes and drinks and when they were served Bridget dragged her gaze from the stunning view and smiled her thanks. But Etienne was looking beyond her right shoulder, his mouth slightly open, his eyes staring.

Bridget turned her head to follow his gaze. A young woman with long, black hair was the only person in the narrow street. She walked away from them, ran quickly up a short flight of steps and disappeared from sight.

When Bridget looked once again at Etienne, his face was a sickly yellow. 'What is it?' she asked. 'What's wrong?' He closed his eyes and shook his head, wiped his forehead with the back of his hand. Bridget waited. He opened his eyes and looked directly at her.

'Nothing, nothing, I am fine. I thought I saw someone I know, someone I used to come to Eze with, but I was wrong. I am o.k.'

They ate their lunch in silence and after some time Etienne asked, 'When you are going home to your husband, Bridget?'

'I don't know. I'm not ready. I haven't figured it out yet.' The tears started in her eyes.

'How long do you think it will take?'

'I don't know, I tell you, I don't know.' She ran from the table, tears streaming down her face.

*

Half an hour later Etienne found her, cold and shivering, in l'Eglise Notre-Dame de l'Assomption. He led her out to the warmth of the sun and sat her on a stone bench. He put his arms round her and held her close. He waited for her to speak and when she did the words came halting and stumbling at first, and then in torrents.

She told him how, for as long as she could remember she'd been overwhelmed by a feeling of loneliness, a certainty that she was impossible to love. She knew this wasn't true. After all, she was married to Matt who loved her and whom she loved in return, and they had a good life. 'But I ran away because, because …' she let the words tail off.

After a few moments she continued. 'I seem fated to run away from people I love,' she said. Ten years previously she'd left her family and friends in Ireland and moved to Birmingham. 'Loneliness is worse,' she assured him, 'when you experience it among your own people. When that happens you feel there's no place in the world for you.'

At first the move seemed to work, but before too long the old feelings of desperation started up again. But she'd met Matt and in the excitement of falling in love and getting married she thought she'd at last left her sadness behind.

Then her contentment leaked away and left her with a terrible emptiness that nothing could fill. She'd found that it wasn't easy to escape the past. 'I think for those who stay put, remain in the same place throughout their lives, past events recede; are crowded out by subsequent events that unfold in the same place. Away from home, the past is frozen in time, becomes crystallized, clear and sharp and impossible to forget,' she said.

'I am not sure I agree, Bridget,' Etienne said, quietly. 'I think this can also happen to those who never leave home.'

*

Interlude

They sat in silence as a young man and women conveyed, with pointed looks, their wish to share the bench.

'I think it's only gorgeous here,' the woman said.

'Yeah, it's pretty cool,' the young man agreed.

'I've always wanted to get married in a hillside church by the sea,' said the woman, flicking her hair away from her face and sliding a glance at the man, 'and this church has something extra that makes it perfect, Eamon.'

'What's that?' asked Eamon.

'You mean you didn't notice?' The young woman was aggrieved.

'Well, I suppose …' Eamon hesitated, playing for time.

'It has my name. It's The Church of the Assumption and sure isn't my name Assumpta?'

'I'd need a better reason than that to travel all the way from Ireland to the South of France to get married,' said Eamon.

'If you loved me you'd want to make my special day perfect,' said Assumpta,'

'Yeah, but it'd be awful expensive, I mean, we'd have to …'

'You're a mean, insensitive pig.' Assumpta gave her hair an angry toss, rose from the bench and ran down the hill towards the main road.

Eamon smiled nervously at Bridget and Etienne, raised his shoulders in a helpless shrug and then raced after his beloved.

'The South of France seems to be overrun by the Irish,' Bridget said, with a wan smile.

*

'Have you told Matt how you feel, Bridget? Etienne asked.

'I've tried, she said, and looked away into the distance. Matt thinks we should start a family,' she said. 'He thinks a baby would help fill the void, he says that if I have my own child I'll never be lonely again. But I think he's wrong. I don't think a child can exert such power.'

She paused for a moment before continuing. 'Surely you shouldn't have a baby to mend your own life,' she appealed to Etienne, 'You shouldn't have a baby for selfish reasons.' Besides she felt she had nothing to give a child. The way she was now she couldn't be a good mother. 'And I want to be a good mother,' she sobbed, and Etienne held her tighter still.

She knew she needed to be by herself, to have time to think and work it out. So every night since her arrival in Nice she'd spent hours writing. She thought if she could write it all out she would send it to Matt and then he'd understand. 'But what I've written is drivel,' she said, despairingly. 'Blathering on about being absorbed into a painting, outpourings about my pathological fear of pregnancy and childbirth even though I'm living in the twenty-first century and have access to all the latest medical advances — the whole thing verges on the mystical, the primitive. If I send these pathetic ramblings to Matt he'll despise me;

Interlude

think I'm worthless or maybe even mad,' she ended with a shuddering sob.

*

'Have a warm bath and rest,' Etienne advised. She'd done as he'd suggested, but stifled by the stuffy room, she rose from the bed, threw open the French window and drew the tiny table onto the balcony. Above the roar of the traffic and the bustle of pedestrians as they rushed to and fro beneath her, she sat and ate the food Etienne had insisted on buying. 'You must keep up your strength and you must keep writing,' he said, as they walked away from the church towards the bus stop. 'You must persevere, Bridget.' But she couldn't bring herself to write that evening: she couldn't think of anything else to say.

As she lay in bed she remembered Etienne's face, shocked and pale, looking beyond her into his past as they sat in the café in Eze. She thought of his brown eyes ringed with laughter lines and wondered what had happened to make a once happy face so sad. She knew with certainty that what he'd experienced allowed him to empathize with her, to comprehend her turmoil and to refuse to judge her.

*

It was an old dream, one she hadn't had for a long time. She was about seven years old and she was alone by the sea. The beach stretched for miles and she ran up and down searching for something, but she didn't know what. The sand grew deeper and deeper, engulfing her shoulders and had almost reached her mouth, when she saw a shimmering figure emerge from the water. The figure came closer and closer but then, as though pulled by an invisible thread, it turned and waded back into the gently lapping waves. The water swelled, then settled, and the figure had gone. She screamed and screamed, begging her mother to come back, but her screams were silenced as her mouth filled with sand.

*

The ringing of the phone woke her. '*Bonjour Bridget,*' Etienne's voice was overly cheerful. 'Today I think we will go to Musée Marc Chagall.'

'I'm still in bed.'

'I'll meet you outside the hotel in one hour.'

'Make it two hours, I need to write.'

'I know you will like Chagall's work,' Etienne assured her as they made their way along the steep incline of the Boulevard de Cimiez.

'How can you be so sure?' Bridget asked

'Because his paintings tell everything there is to know.'

When they entered the main gallery Etienne wandered off, leaving Bridget to discover Chagall undisturbed. The scale of the twelve paintings depicting scenes from the Old Testament was awesome, the richness of colour breathtaking. Bridget allowed her gaze to pan round the room, wanting to take in everything at once. Dizzied by the rainbow of colour and the grandeur of the artist's vision she

Interlude

closed her eyes and then slowly opened them again. She was looking at a gigantic painting of Adam and Eve's expulsion from the Garden of Eden.

Swathes of deepest blue swept across a verdant background. Figures — celestial, human and animal —— freed from all ties, floated in the lush landscape. The sacred and profane mingled freely. The banishing angel and the banished couple were rendered in blinding white, with Eve's breasts tinged pink and her flowing hair a carnal red. A lascivious, yellow goat emerged from rich vegetation and a crimson cockerel eyed the angel with angry disdain. In the foreground, what Bridget took to be a dazzling multi-coloured tree of knowledge (but might well have been a burning bush) promised infinite pleasure.

She stood transfixed, captivated by the vibrant eroticism of Chagall's free-flowing world and was comforted by the fact that out of banishment and rejection the artist had created a world full of possibility; a world where we can free ourselves from constraints, where it might be possible to determine our own destiny.

Etienne stood back and watched as she circled the gallery, pausing for several minutes at each painting before she moved on to the next. When she'd completed the circuit he approached and, taking her by the elbow, led her to a smaller hexagonal room. 'I brought you here particularly to see these pictures,' he said. 'Take as long as you like. I shall wait for you in the garden café.'

Song of Songs was Chagall's inspiration for the five large paintings that dominated the room. He had used a palette of pinks and reds that imbued the space with an ardent, sensual glow. Figures and buildings were set free to float at will, some right-side up, others upside down. A bride, dressed in virginal white stood with her groom, elongated and upright, towering over their world, whilst at the same time they lay at their own feet, entwined and unashamed in blissful abandon. A womb-shaped tree drifted across the landscape, its curving branches offering repose to a nude female who pleasured herself as a donkey peeped, lewdly, from behind another tree.

As Bridget gazed at Chagall's floating domain where land and water combined to create an unfettered world, tiny particles of ice seemed to melt in her veins, allowing the blood to flow freely.

She thought of Joyce's Mollie Bloom, languishing in her bed, pleasuring herself as she remembered the past with pleasure. Chagall, she realized, had created a visual stream of consciousness, had painted human thought and awareness, fragments of remembering — random and disconnected — flitting across the fluidscape of memory, where the past and present coalesce to help create the future. He showed how what we remember stirs the imagination and creates our longings, our desires.

She thought of the nights spent in her hotel room writing furiously in an attempt to reconcile events in her past with the present. The past, she realized, is the fuel of the future, and she needed to use it, without fear, if she and Matt were to go on together.

She hurried outside to find Etienne.

They sat in the garden café, sipping their drinks. *"En art tout comme dans la vie, tout est possible pourvu que l'amour y soit a la base,"* Etienne told her — "In art as in life, everything is possible, as long as it is based upon love". 'That is what Chagall believed, that is what he said.'

'Do you agree?' Bridget asked.

'I find I must agree,' Etienne said. 'If I do not believe that love makes the seemingly impossible possible I see no reason to go on.'

*

Later that evening she walked alone to the internet café on rue St. Vincent. The café was filled with young people from all over Europe and from America and Australia. She sipped a glass of water as she waited for a terminal. When she finally logged on there were no new messages for her. She stared at the screen for a few moments, logged off and hurried back to her hotel.

She wrote quickly and without hesitation, filling the pages with great sprawling, looping letters. Words poured from her, an unstoppable haemorrhaging of thoughts and feelings until, finally, in the small hours of the morning, exhausted and drained, she lay on the bed and fell asleep.

*

She woke early, showered, and without waiting for breakfast, left the hotel and hurried towards the railway station. She cursed silently when she saw that the internet café was closed. She had half an hour to wait until it opened so she went across to the station and bought an orange juice and a croissant.

The young, bearded man who unlocked the door smiled warmly, *'Bonjour Madame,* you are in a hurry this morning, you have important business?' Bridget brushed passed him and stood impatiently as he switched on the terminals. She logged on, entered her email address and waited. Still no new messages. She clicked on Matt's address and started to type.

Sixty minutes later she emerged and returned to the hotel. She went to her room, draped the 'do not disturb' sign on the door handle, closed the window and drew the curtains. She rang the receptionist and asked her to hold her calls.

*

Etienne rang the hotel three times before midday and each time was told that Madame was not taking any calls. He sat on the steps of the Holiday Inn and watched the hotel door. When two o'clock past and there was still no sign of Bridget he tried phoning again. This time the receptionist put him through. 'Bridget I've been so worried, you would not take my calls and you have not left the hotel all day.'

Bridget said something about a 'bird' and a 'worm' that he didn't understand but her voice was not sad. 'I will see you at eight o'clock this evening, Etienne', she said. 'I will treat you to dinner at The Westminster. I have something I want to tell you.'

Sometime later she walked onto the balcony, checked that Etienne wasn't watching from the steps opposite, left the hotel and returned to the internet café by the station.

She sat before the screen, hardly daring to log on, typed her email address, then her password. She took several deep breaths before clicking the mouse. There was just one new email. From Matt. It was only 3KB in length. Her upper lip was damp with sweat. She took another deep breath. She moved the arrow to Matt's name, closed her eyes, clicked the mouse, then opened her eyes and read the message.

*

She looked in dismay at the few clothes hanging in the wardrobe. When she'd left Birmingham a week before, she'd thrown a few things into a bag and now found that she had nothing to wear for a special night out.

She drew on her black jeans and the only top she hadn't yet worn, also black. It was a warm evening so she'd simply drape her jade pashmina round her shoulders. She wore silver earrings and a silver pendant that Matt had given her for her last birthday. She checked herself in the mirror and was not displeased with the image that looked back at her. The black outfit accentuated her slim figure; the blue-green of the pashmina drew out the colour of her eyes and enhanced her pale-blonde hair.

Etienne was waiting for her outside the hotel. As they walked towards the front they passed the shops that displayed the posters of Sarkozy. 'He reminds me of a bird of prey,' said Bridget, with a slight shudder. 'Do you think he'll be elected, Etienne?'

'The French will never vote for a male version of Margaret Thatcher,' Etienne said with unusual force.

'The British did,' Bridget said.

'And they have suffered for their foolishness. They work the longest hours in Europe and they are involved in an illegal war. No, the French will not allow such a man to change their way of life.'

*

A waiter in an olive-green apron greeted them. Etienne assured him that they had indeed booked and he led them to the table by the umbrella plant where Bridget had sat on her first evening in Nice. As Etienne ordered the food and wine she glanced round the restaurant: as on her previous visit all of the tables were occupied by couples or groups.

'You look very beautiful tonight, Bridget,' Etienne said, breaking in on her reverie.

'Thank you, Etienne.'

'You have something to tell me.'

'Yes, I have something I want to tell you.'

They waited in silence as the waiter served a fish soup, pungent with garlic and herbs.

'I kept writing as you said I should.' Bridget hesitated, broke off a piece of bread and took a

Interlude

mouthful of soup. Etienne didn't say anything. He concentrated on eating.

'And, finally, I found the courage to write about something … something I've tried so hard to forget, to bury. She took a sip of water and continued. 'I was about seven years old, I think, and one day I woke up and my mother wasn't there.'

'Was she ill? he asked. 'Had she been taken to hospital?'

'No, she'd left. Just left.' Bridget steadied her voice before continuing. 'The person who was my whole world had gone, vanished. Every morning before that I knew Mammy was there — somewhere in the house. Every day she kissed me awake, and I would dress in the clean clothes she'd put out the night before. She made my breakfast, gave me my packed lunch, my P.E. kit, walked me to school and kissed me goodbye.'

The waiter cleared the soup tureen and the dishes from the table, replacing them with a casserole of coq au van and a plate of mixed vegetables. Etienne poured two glasses of wine.

'When I came out of school Mammy would be waiting for me, every day. Then we'd go home and I'd change my clothes and I'd drink orange juice and Mammy would have tea and we'd eat a slice of apple tart or chocolate cake and I'd go outside and play until she called me in for dinner. After dinner I would have a bath and Mammy made sure I cleaned my neck and my ears. And Daddy would read me a story and they'd both kiss me goodnight and I'd go to sleep and then it would start again the next day.

Bridget stopped for a moment, sipped her wine and then continued. 'Except when I woke one day she'd gone. And my father was mad with worry. He told me that Mammy had gone to the country to look after her sick mother, but I didn't believe him. I knew she wouldn't go to visit my Granny without telling me and, besides, every night after he put me to bed he sat at the kitchen table and cried. He made a terrible noise which frightened me. He sounded like next door's dog when they wouldn't let him in, when they shut him out for a long time. And I wanted to cry out too. Being separated from Mammy was like being separated from my own skin and the pain was unendurable. But I didn't cry because there was no one to hear me. Her voice shook and Etienne kept his gaze averted.

'I am sorry, Bridget,' he said.

*

They walked along the Promenade, crowded as usual with pedestrians, skaters and joggers. 'I think Chagall was wrong about love,' Bridget said. 'Love doesn't make everything possible. My mother loved me, but her need to escape was more powerful than her maternal love.'

'That is a harsh judgement, Bridget.'

'The world is a harsh place for a child, Etienne. Children have no control over their world; they're at the mercy of adults.'

Interlude

Etienne led her to a seat overlooking the sea that pounded in the dark below. 'But your mother returned,' he said.

'Yes. One morning I woke up and she was there. I thought I was dreaming. I'd been dreaming for a long time that she would come back. Every morning I expected her to be there and one morning she was. But for me she'd been gone an eternity. For a child each day is a lifetime. And no one ever talked about it. No one ever said why she went, so I thought it must be my fault, that I'd been so bold I'd driven my mother away. And I was always scared that I would do something to drive her away again.'

*

They sat in silence, listening to the sounds of the waves rattling the pebbles on the beach. Etienne spoke quietly. 'But Chagall was right after all, Bridget, love made the seemingly impossible, possible. 'Your mother loved you so much she couldn't stay away.'

When Bridget spoke again her voice was flat and lifeless. 'But she'd stolen the most vital thing;' she said, 'the certainty that she loved me. When you're not certain of your mother's love you feel worthless and afraid — always afraid and always lonely.'

Etienne waited a long time before answering. 'Perhaps life makes too great demands of women.' he said, 'Perhaps sometimes they need to escape, need an interlude so that they can recoup and then carry on. Perhaps your mother needed such an interlude.'

Bridget stood and walked to the sea wall. She watched the line of white foam curl onto the beach and then recede. Etienne followed her. 'You have told Matt?' he asked.

'Yes.' she said. Yes, I've finally told him. When Mammy left I didn't tell anyone, not even Marie Murphy, my best friend. She kept asking me where Mammy was and I repeated the lie that Daddy had told me, that she'd gone to the country to look after my sick Granny. But still I was sure everyone knew what had happened; that they pointed me out as the girl who'd been abandoned by her mother. I was so ashamed that Mammy had left, so sure that it was my fault and terrified that I would never see her again.'

Bridget handed Etienne a sheet of paper. 'Read it,' she said. He walked towards a streetlight and scanned the sheet.

Arriving on the 06.35 flight tomorrow. Have booked two tickets on the 11.15 to Birmingham on Monday. I'll come to your hotel. Matt.

'Have you told him … everything?'

'How do you know there's more to tell?'

'It's not so difficult Bridget — you have the look, what we call in France, '*un regard intérieur*', 'the inward gaze' which tells the world that for the woman, only the child in her womb exists.'

'It's not certain yet and, besides, I want to be with him when I tell him.'

'I am happy for you, Bridget. I am happy that your interlude has ended well.'

'Perhaps it's too soon to tell.'

Interlude

'I feel that, in your case, Chagall is right'. Etienne took her hand, kissed it lightly, then turned and walked away.

Bridget stood looking after him, keeping track of the light-grey jacket as it weaved in and out of the throng on the Promenade, until finally it disappeared into the night.

*

She hurried back to the hotel. She would ring Matt, she thought. She needed to hear his voice, husky with affection and longing.

The receptionist smiled at her. 'It is good that you befriended Monsieur Henry during your stay in Nice, Madame,' he said.

'You know Etienne?' Bridget was surprised.

'He is well-known in Nice, Madame.'

'Why is that?' Bridget asked.

'You do not know his story, Madame?'

'No, no I don't,' she said and an image of Etienne's face crumbled with pain as they sat in the café in Eze, came back to her.

Etienne and Françoise had come to Nice on their honeymoon. They had always holidayed in Nice as children, their families had made the short journey from their homes in Marseilles every August. They loved the place and they couldn't think of anywhere else they wanted to be.

'But Françoise, she had problems, Madame, she did not enjoy good health; she …' He frowned, and with a shrug of his shoulders he left the sentence hanging in the air. 'Two years after their wedding she left home, disappeared without a word,' he continued. 'The police they were, as usual, useless,' he said with another shrug. 'They said that an adult had the right to absent herself, that it was not a crime. As though we do not know this!' Etienne hired a private detective but it was hopeless. Françoise was never found.

There had been many supposed sightings; the last in Nice, a year ago. 'So Monsieur Henry comes to Nice every holiday. He wanders the streets in the hope of finding his Françoise, Madame. *C'est tragique*,' the receptionist said, as he handed her the key. 'It is tragic, Madame, very tragic.'

*

Bridget couldn't sleep so she opened the French window and dragged a chair onto the narrow balcony. The din of the traffic had died down, allowing the city a brief respite before the morning clamour started up again. A few late-night stragglers hurried along the street below.

It was difficult to take in what the receptionist had told her, difficult to understand why Etienne had not shared his sadness with her. But she'd been so absorbed in her own turmoil that she'd given him little opportunity; had given little thought to him or anyone else.

She'd panicked; left home because she thought she might be pregnant, because she was terrified of what that might mean, not just for herself, she realized now, but also for her baby.

Interlude

Without intending to she'd hurt people who cared for her; left Matt alone and frantic, and accepted Etienne's support and friendship without considering the cost to either of them.

She thought of her mother whom she'd judged so harshly and wondered if she, like herself, had been frightened of motherhood. Bridget was an only child so it was possible. Maybe her mother had run away because of pressure to have another child. Bridget would never know and it was too late now to pick at the scab of a wound she supposed had long since healed for her mother.

She wanted to believe, as Etienne had suggested, that her mother had loved her so much she couldn't stay away. She offered a silent thank you and asked her mother's forgiveness for doubting her.

*

She would wait until morning to telephone Matt. Tonight she would dedicate to Etienne who'd been willing to draw on his own pain to help a stranger negotiate the turbulent waters of a difficult interlude.

She thought of Chagall's paintings with their brilliant colours and their message of hope. She heard Etienne's soft voice, filled with a desperate conviction, when he said that he believed Chagall's pronouncement that love made the seemingly impossible, possible.

She hoped, fervently, that Chagall was right.

ORDER FORM

To order further copies of GILDED SHADOWS please contact:

Tia Publishing,
37 Chesterwood Road
Birmingham
B13 0QG.

Telephone: 0121 2425123

Email   tia.publishing@yahoo.com

Or visit: www.maryrochford.co.uk

Tia Publishing